British Army Yearb

Combat Brigades – Operations – Ceremonial – Future Plans

LEFT: Gurkha soldiers from Nepal have served in the British Army for more than 200 years. (MOD/CROWN COPYRIGHT)

BELOW: The Irish Guards received new regimental colours from King Charles III at Windsor Castle in June 2024. (MOD/CROWN COPYRIGHT)

ISBN: 978 1 80282 997 6
Editor: Tim Ripley
Data and photo research: Fergus Ripley
Senior editor, specials: Roger Mortimer
Email: roger.mortimer@keypublishing.com
Cover Design: Steve Donovan
Design: SJmagic DESIGN SERVICES, India
Advertising Sales Manager: Sam Clark
Email: sam.clark@keypublishing.com
Tel: 01780 755131
Advertising Production: Becky Antoniades
Email: Rebecca.antoniades@keypublishing.com

SUBSCRIPTION/MAIL ORDER
Key Publishing Ltd,
PO Box 300, Stamford,
Lincs, PE9 1NA
Tel: 01780 480404
Subscriptions email: subs@keypublishing.com
Mail Order email: orders@keypublishing.com
Website: www.keypublishing.com/shop

PUBLISHING
Group CEO and Publisher:
Adrian Cox

Published by
Key Publishing Ltd, PO Box 100, Stamford,
Lincs, PE9 1XQ
Tel: 01780 755131
Website: www.keypublishing.com

PRINTING
Precision Colour Printing Ltd, Haldane,
Halesfield 1, Telford, Shropshire. TF7 4QQ

DISTRIBUTION
Seymour Distribution Ltd, 2 Poultry Avenue,
London, EC1A 9PU
Enquiries Line: 02074 294000.

Welcome

British Army Yearbook 2024

ABOVE: Britain's infantry leads the way.
(MOD/CROWN COPYRIGHT)

Welcome to the fourth edition of the *British Army Yearbook* - your essential guide to the British Army. This annual publication aims to provide a wide readership with an update on what the army of the United Kingdom has been doing over the past year and its future direction, as well as looking back at its illustrious history.

The past year has seen the British Army step up to the plate to support NATO as it confronts Russia across Europe. More than 16,000 British soldiers headed to Europe during the first six months of 2024 to test NATO's war plans and we look in detail how Exercise Steadfast Defender 2024 played out.

This saw British troops training in Estonia, Poland, Germany, and elsewhere across Europe, carrying out armoured drills, building bridges to cross rivers, and launching simulated helicopter-borne raids. Nothing like this has been seen in a generation and we profile each of the major phases of the exercise.

As well as playing its role in NATO's deterrent mission, the British Army continues to work on operations around the world to defend Britain and its allies. We look at the continuing role of the British Army to help the Ukrainians fight off Russian attacks. British troops are highly active in the Middle East, defending

RIGHT: A new generation of British Army officers graduate from the Royal Military Academy Sandhurst.
(MOD/CROWN COPYRIGHT)

ABOVE: It is 25 years since the British Army led NATO peacekeepers into Kosovo and ended the brutal Serb occupation of the province. (MOD/CROWN COPYRIGHT)

LEFT: The RAF's new A400M Atlas is now fully cleared to drop Paratroopers of 16 Air Assault Brigade into action. (MOD/CROWN COPYRIGHT)

BELOW: Tim Ripley on tour in Iraq with the King's Own Scottish Borderers regiment. (TIM RIPLEY)

coalition bases against drone attacks and helping the Royal Air Force air drop humanitarian aid to Gaza.

This June saw the British Army say goodbye to General Sir Patrick Sanders after two years at the helm as chief of the general staff. He tells us about the challenges facing the British Army and the tasks awaiting his successor, General Sir Roly Walker.

In June, Britain paid tribute to the veterans of D-Day, and we look back at the Normandy landings 80 years ago. We also profile the role played by the British Army in Radfan 60 years ago and in Kosovo in 1999.

The British Army continues to evolve to meet new threats and challenges. In *British Army Yearbook 2024* we take a close look at each of the British Army's frontline brigades,

profiling their key regiments, equipment, and distinguished history.

We take a close look at the work to provide the British Army with 21st century weapons and equipment and examine how the rapidly changing nature of warfare is impacting it.

General Walker faces huge challenges as the new head of the British Army, and we lay out some of the major issues that will land on his desk over the coming year.

We hope the *British Army Yearbook 2024* is an informative read and stimulates further interest in the British Army as it moves to keep ahead of the latest trends in warfare.

Tim Ripley
Editor
July 2024

General Sanders Talks

Chief of the General Staff Signs Off

RIGHT: In 2022 General Sanders set the British Army a tough challenge to get ready for possible further conflict in Europe. (MOD/CROWN COPYRIGHT)

Britain's top soldier hung up his uniform for the final time in June, 2024, after nearly 40 years of service. General Sir Patrick Sanders had been chief of the general staff for two years and had headed Strategic Command, giving him more than four and half years of four-star governance.

The general commanded his battalion with distinction in Iraq and then led a brigade to Afghanistan, so he was recognised as one of the British Army's foremost leaders of his generation.

He had a reputation for blunt talking, and on several occasions had embarrassed his political masters by 'saying it, how it is'. Earlier this year he talked to the International Armoured Vehicle Conference at Twickenham in his last major public address before retiring.

"At [my] Royal United Services Institute [speech] in 2022, I talked about a 1937 moment and the need to mobilise," said Sanders. "Not everyone agreed.

"[When] I launched the British Army's Operation Mobilise, it would be our main effort, underwriting the priority to support Ukraine," he said. "At the DSEI [exhibition in London's Docklands in 2023], I declared that we are now a pre-war generation. Our predecessors failed to perceive the implications of the so-called July Crisis in 1914 and stumbled into the most ghastly of wars. We cannot afford to make the same mistake today. Ukraine really matters."

According to the general: "[Ukraine] is the principal pressure point on a fragile world order that our enemies wish to dismantle. I use that term with care, noting that the definition encompasses those who actively oppose or are hostile to our interests.

BELOW: British Army training teams are operating around the world with allies and partners as part of its continuous engagement concept to head off conflict and instability. (MOD/CROWN COPYRIGHT)

Wilhelm's memorable and gleeful remark that "dreadnoughts have no wheels" reminds us that the enemy gets a vote. Land will always matter because it's where people live. You can't lead NATO from the flanks, and if we want agency in the way in which our big blind could be spent, we must be able to credibly fight and win wars on land.

"We need an army designed to expand rapidly to enable the first echelon, resource the second echelon, and train and equip the citizen army that must follow," said the general. "Within the next three years, it must be credible to talk of a British Army of 120,000, folding in our reserve and strategic reserve. But this is not enough. As the chairman of the NATO Military Committee warned just last week, and as the Swedish government has done, preparing Sweden for entry to NATO, taking preparatory steps to enable placing our societies on a war footing when »

LEFT: General Sanders first joined the British Army in 1984 and served in all levels of command until being appointed chief of the general staff in June 2022. (MOD/CROWN COPYRIGHT)

BELOW: The Royal Artillery is receiving new Archer 155mm self propelled guns as part of a £41bn modernisation drive by the British Army. (MOD/CROWN COPYRIGHT)

This war is not merely about the black soil of the Donbass, nor the re-establishment of a Russian empire, it's about defeating our system and way of life politically, psychologically, and symbolically. How we respond as the pre-war generation will reverberate through history. Ukrainian bravery is buying time, for now. Ukraine really matters. I cannot overstate it."

Operation Mobilise was an important development, said Sanders, because: "it focused the British Army on delivery, making the most of the army we have to help deter Russia. Allied to the Field Army's *How We Fight 2026* publication, we have driven profound advances in our thinking, training, equipment, productivity, and our relationship with industry. We are the most productive army in Europe and the rapid deployment of SACEUR's Strategic Reserve Force to Kosovo [in October 2023] evidences the substance of readiness."

Sanders said the British Army intended to deploy 16,000 troops on 11 NATO-facing training events spanning 10 countries, including 1,000 armoured and protected mobility vehicles in the first half of 2024. "In many respects, Exercise Steadfast Defender marks the summit of Operation Mobilise, embedding a culture of readiness into the fabric of tomorrow's British Army," he said.

Thirdly, he highlighted the NATO Force Model (NFM). "The British Army's delivery of forces for multi-domain operations must be anchored to NATO," said Sanders. "As the secretary of state noted last week, NATO is our pre-eminent partner and the NFM provides our star to steer by. As chief of the general staff, I must deliver the British Army that NATO needs. And I call-out those who extrapolate our maritime heritage too far, judging that our NATO contribution can be largely limited to the maritime and air domains. Kaiser

ABOVE: Getting out and about to meet his soldiers has been an important part of General Sanders' job, as head of the British Army. (MOD/CROWN COPYRIGHT)

BELOW: Drones are playing a increasing role in British Army operations. (MOD/CROWN COPYRIGHT)

needed are now not merely desirable, but essential.

"We will not be immune and as the pre-war generation we must similarly prepare - and that is a whole-of-nation undertaking," he said. "Ukraine brutally illustrates that regular armies start wars; citizen armies win them. But we've been here before, and workforce alone does not create capability. This last weekend, *The Times* highlighted the British Army's dwindling numbers. It reminded us that over the last 30 years, the British Army has been halved in size; in the last 12 years, we've absorbed a 28% reduction. Despite that narrative, applications to join the British Army are the highest in six years. Our nation's youth are as ready to serve, to seek adventure, to find where they belong, and to better themselves as they ever were.

"Some perceive a death knell for armoured vehicles in the fleeting, high-pitch buzz of a First Person View (FPV) piloted 'kamikaze' drone as it delivers a shaped charge into an armoured vehicle," he commented. "There are some who predict a 21st century 'Revolution in Military Affairs' by virtue of drones, signalling the obsolescence of the tank, for example. The tactics of survivability are coming back to the fore. Armour plating is the last bastion, the innermost layer of the so-called onion of survivability. Dispersion, concealment, and deception are as relevant as ever."

The general highlighted the British Army's modernisations efforts, saying it will result in over 1,200 armoured vehicles flowing into it over the next five years. Ajax is already in the Field Army; with operationally deployable vehicles arriving at scale this year. "[It is] an AH-64 [Apache attack helicopter] on tracks, it is without equal across NATO, and we will have a total of 589 platforms," he said. "The 623 UK Boxer will start fielding in 2025, bringing proven mobility and survivability to our Brigade Combat Teams – but we want more - and we are now setting out the case for the acquisition of additional variants. The first Challenger 3 prototypes are being put through trials in the UK and Germany and I'm delighted that Prototype 1 is already being readied for live firing, on time.

"But armour is simply part of the equation; the real alchemy of land power is the integration of armoured platforms into a much broader, combined arms system," said Sanders. "A system of manoeuvre, fires, assault, and support. The British Army's version is 'Combined Arms Manoeuvre', but others are available. Armoured forces are at the heart of this system because everything from command and control, to unmanned aerial systems, combat engineers, artillery, and close combat troops must be survivable. We're investing over a billion pounds in our new Mobile Fires Platform as the long-term replacement for AS90 [155mm self-propelled guns] and the interim Archer capability. Pending HM Treasury approvals, the first Mobile Fires Platform platforms should start flowing into the Field Army in 2029.

"The context has changed, and a lack of strategic means will ruthlessly undermine the ends we seek," he said.

ABOVE: Improving recruiting and retention has been a top priority for General Sanders to ensure the British Army has the skilled soldiers it needs.
(MOD/CROWN COPYRIGHT)

LEFT: Training Ukrainian soldiers has been a priority mission for the British Army since June 2022.
(MOD/CROWN COPYRIGHT)

"We must reframe our strategic approach and be clear-eyed that Russia is spending nearly 40% of public expenditure on defence. And we know that we need it not only to be the most lethal British Army in Europe, but to attract and retain the outstanding talent that has chosen to serve.

"Let me finish where I started, today's strategic context demands an enduring ability to deliver integrated armoured forces," concluded the general. "We are the pre-war generation and Ukraine is the vital ground. Back in 2022, the British Army mobilised in response to this context generating a readiness and productivity dividend that you will see this year across the continent as part of Exercise Steadfast Defender."

Soldiers, Regiments, and Kit

In the News

General Sir Roly Walker takes over

RIGHT: The new chief of the general staff is a Grenadier Guard, who has seen extensive service with Britain's special forces. (MOD/CROWN COPYRIGHT)

THE BRITISH Army has a new head, after General Sir Roly Walker took over General Sir Patrick Sanders on June 15, 2024.

"Roly's wealth of operational experience and previous appointments make him very well suited to lead the British Army as we continue to modernise our armed forces to meet the threats and challenges in a more contested and dangerous world," said chief of the defence staff Admiral Sir Tony Radakin, after General Walker's new appointment was first announced last December.

General Walker said: "I am absolutely thrilled to be appointed as the next chief of the general staff. It has always been a tremendous honour to lead our nation's soldiers, so the chance to serve them once again, and in this role, is the highest of privileges. It also carries great responsibility, which I promise to discharge to the best of my abilities. Our soldiers, and those who support them, deserve nothing less.

"My task will be to build on the successes of my predecessor and friend, Patrick, and lead the British Army forward on an ambitious modernisation journey that means we are fitter, faster for the challenges of the future. There is plenty to be excited about. The scene is set. We know our part in defence's plan. I'm looking forward to starting."

General Walker was commissioned into the Irish Guards in 1993 and served with the UK's special forces from 1997. He commanded the Grenadier Guards in 2009, being promoted to the general staff four years later. He has commanded at company, squadron, battle group, brigade, and special forces group levels, variously in Northern Ireland, Afghanistan, Iraq, as well as joint command of operations across Europe, the broader Middle East, Africa, and South America. Prior to leading the British Army, he was deputy chief of defence staff (Military Strategy & Operations) at the Ministry of Defence.

RIGHT: General Walker took over as head of the British Army on June 15, 2024. (MOD/CROWN COPYRIGHT)

Paratroopers dropped over France to mark D-Day 80

TO MARK the 80th anniversary of D Day, three Airbus A400M Atlas aircraft have dropped Paratroopers of 16 Air Assault Brigade over Sannerville, in Normandy, mirroring the actions of RAF Dakota aircraft 80 years ago.

The event marked the first public display of the A400M's paratrooper deployment capabilities, and saw paratroopers jump from aircraft's two side doors.

The A400M, based at RAF Brize Norton, led a formation followed by United States Air Force Lockheed Martin C-130 Hercules and a Belgian Air Force A400M, which both dropped paratroopers from their respective armed forces.

On the night of June 5, 1944, hundreds of Dakotas took off from airfields across England. These aircraft carried thousands of paratroopers, tasked with securing key sites behind enemy lines. Their mission was critical to the success of the overall invasion, as they aimed to disrupt German defences, capture

strategic bridges, and establish defensive positions.

The paratroopers faced intense anti-aircraft fire, navigational challenges, and perilous landings in the dark, often being scattered over wide areas. Despite these difficulties, their efforts significantly contributed to the eventual success of the Normandy landings.

Since entering RAF service in 2014, the A400M has played a pivotal role in several operations. It was a central part of the UK's hurricane relief efforts in the Caribbean and as part of the military response to the COVID-19 pandemic it transported patients, equipment, and vaccines. Atlas also played an important role in the evacuation of refugees from Afghanistan and Sudan, and most recently has air-dropped aid to Gaza.

ABOVE: Modern paratroopers of 16 Air Assault Brigade recreated the historic jump into Normandy in 1944 by their World War Two predecessors. (MOD/CROWN COPYRIGHT)

LEFT: D-Day on June 6, 1944, opened with British and American airborne forces landing by parachute and glider to seize strategic positions across Normandy. (MOD/CROWN COPYRIGHT)

Soldier wins Gladiator

A BRITISH Army major has won the reboot of classic TV show Gladiators.

In March, the 35-year-old, Major Finlay Anderson, from Edinburgh, battled through to win the epic test of strength and endurance.

He went into the final Eliminator challenge level on points with Ministry of Defence civil servant Wesley Malé, against whom he had failed to claw back an 11 second disadvantage by a split-second in the quarter-final. It was only the second time he wasn't behind going into the last challenge.

"The moment I crashed through the finish line I was looking directly at my family and friends. I looked them in the eye and gave them a wave while still on [the] rope. It was pretty wild."

Finlay is officer commanding of Alpha Company, 2nd Battalion, The Royal Regiment of Scotland.

LEFT: Gladiators, ready? Major Finlay Anderson certainly was. (MOD/CROWN COPYRIGHT)

Return of the 'CAT'

BRITISH CHALLENGER 2 crews came second in a test of the skills of NATO tanks in Latvia in May. Members of the Queen's Royal Hussars travelled down from their temporary base in Estonia to take part in the famous Canadian Army Trophy – dubbed the CAT – which was last held in Grafenwoehr, Germany in 1991.

The contest has been revived to promote lethality, training, and interaction between allies. Alongside the UK and the host nation, teams from Italy, Germany, Norway, Poland, and Spain also took part. After a testing series of static and on-the-move shoots, the cavalrymen finished second on the podium,

between winners Canada and ahead of Italy.

After a 33 year absence, NATO's tank gunnery competition was successfully rejuvenated in 2024 at the Ādaži training ground in Latvia with the support of the Canadian presence in the country. It was a close competition, said the organisers.

RIGHT: Challenger 2 tank crews of The Queen's Royal Hussars secured second place in the prestigious Canadian Army Trophy in May 2024. (@RYSZARDJONSKI)

Challenger Imminent

BRITISH ARMY soldiers are a step closer to getting their hands on their new main battle tank, as the latest Challenger 3 prototype has finished production in Telford.

RIGHT: Eight prototypes of the new Challenger 3 are now undergoing extensive testing before the main battle tanks move to full production. (RBSL)

The latest of eight Challenger 3 prototypes rolled off the Rheinmetall BAE Systems Land (RBSL) factory production line in Telford in April.

The first prototype is already showing its capabilities on trials. All prototypes will be tested under operational conditions to validate their performance and make refinements, before another 140 are built and delivered to the British Army.

The British Army's director of programmes, Major General Jon Swift said:

"Challenger 3 will be at the heart of the British Army's armoured brigade combat teams, alongside Ajax and Boxer, and is critical to the army's warfighting capability and the UK's contribution to NATO. The delivery of these prototype vehicles, the first of which has already started trials, marks a significant milestone on the army's modernisation journey."

Royal AAC

KING CHARLES III has officially handed over the role of colonel-in-chief of the Army Air Corps (AAC) to the Prince of Wales at a ceremony and joint engagement held at the Army Aviation Centre and Army Flying Museum, Middle Wallop, in Hampshire.

The change was originally announced by Buckingham Palace in August 2023. The role was previously held by King Charles III, as Prince of Wales, for 31 years.

AAC Soldiers have been wearing the distinctive blue beret with pride since their formation in 1957. They fly British Army aircraft, such as the Boeing AH-64E Apache attack helicopter, to deliver hard-hitting and effective support to ground forces during the key stages of battle.

During his visit, King Charles III unveiled a plaque commemorating the arrival of the first Apache AH1 helicopter in the Army Flying Museum. He then took the short walk across the airfield to the Middle Wallop control tower where, in front of an Apache, he was met by his son to officially hand over the role of colonel-in-chief.

ABOVE: King Charles III has handed over the role of colonel-in-chief of the Army Air Corps (AAC) to his eldest son, Prince William. (MOD/CROWN COPYRIGHT)

Anglo German 155mm Collaboration

BRITAIN HAS reached a deal with Germany to develop the Royal Artillery's next generation of self-propelled guns.

Prime Minister Rishi Sunak and Chancellor Olaf Scholz announced a new collaboration with Germany on the Remote-Controlled Howitzer 155mm (RCH 155) 52 calibre wheeled artillery systems in April 2024.

The aim is to deliver RCH 155 into service this decade. It will equip Royal Artillery gunners with a world-class close support artillery system to deliver lethal and decisive effect for ground warfare across the span of operations.

RCH 155 delivers increased range and accuracy for artillery engagements, a high rate-of-fire of up to nine rounds-per-minute and possesses

a powerful blend of tactical and operational mobility.

Lieutenant General Dame Sharon Nesmith, the then deputy chief of the general staff, said: "RCH 155 will provide a world class 155mm self-propelled artillery gun system to the

Royal Artillery – an excellent strategic fit with the British Army of the future."

A joint assessment and qualification plan will exploit the combined capabilities of test and trials centres in the UK and Germany, enabling faster delivery at less cost.

LEFT: Britain and Germany are working to develop the RCH 155 as the Royal Artillery's new 155mm self-propelled gun. (MOD/CROWN COPYRIGHT)

NATO Steps Up

Steadfast Defender 2024

During the first half of 2024, 16,000 British soldiers joined allies from 32 NATO nations in a series of exercises across Europe to test war plans to defend the continent. NATO dubbed these exercises Steadfast Defender 2024.

Adopted at the 2023 Vilnius NATO Summit, they were to be the first large-scale test of NATO's new regional defence plans in case of a major Russian attack on Europe.

The aim of Steadfast Defender 2024 was to demonstrate NATO's ability to deploy forces rapidly from North America and other parts of the alliance to reinforce the defence of Europe. It also showed that NATO could conduct and sustain complex, multi-domain operations over several months, across thousands of kilometres, from the High North to central and eastern Europe, and in any conditions.

It was intended to be a clear demonstration of NATO's transatlantic unity and strength and the alliance's determination to continue to do all that is necessary to protect all its members, its values, and the rules-based international order.

Steadfast Defender 2024 was not a single exercise, but a series of inter-linked training events that tested key headquarters and units in the new war plans.

The series concluded on May 31, 2024, after four months of intensive, pan-alliance training. More than

90,000 military personnel, more than 50 ships, more than 80 aircraft flying hundreds of sorties, and more than 1,100 combat vehicles from all 32 NATO member states were involved in the exercise. Training focused on promoting readiness across all domains and at all levels of command from strategic, to operational, to tactical.

"Exercise Steadfast Defender 2024 demonstrated the incredible strength of the transatlantic bond between NATO Allies in Europe and those in North America," said the Supreme Allied Commander Europe

(SACEUR) General Christopher G Cavoli. "The highly-complex military activities conducted over the course of this exercise have demonstrated that this alliance is capable and ready to conduct our core mission of collective defence."

The exercise was executed in two parts. Part one was a maritime-focused live exercise that involved various headquarters rehearsing the strategic deployment of forces from North America to continental Europe. Part two was

BRITISH ARMY IN STEADFAST DEFENDER 2024

#STEADFASTDEFENDER24
#STRONGERTOGETHER

The British Army is committed to European security. Training operations build to their highest peak in 2024, reinforcing land forces' utility and centrality to defending Europe.

16,000 Troops
6 months of events
1 set of shared values - #WeAreNATO

STEADFAST DETERRENCE 24
1 (UK) Div HQ will validate as the 2* Land Component Command, in Stavanger Norway.

BRILLIANT JUMP 1
NATO Response Force 2024 Alert Exercise. Joint Force Command - Brunssum will issue orders to stand up forces in line with the Crisis Response Measures.

POLISH DRAGON 24
A Very High Readiness Joint Task Force (Land) Live Exercise under direction of the Polish Corps. It will include a Distinguished Visitor's Day for Exercise Steadfast Defender.

BRILLIANT JUMP 2
Lead elements of NATO Response Force 2024 Alert Exercise will deploy to Poland to conduct Reception, Staging and Onward Movement, assembly and connectivity.

NORDIC RESPONSE 24
Aviation Task Force 2 and Commando Helicopter Force assets will support 3 Commando Brigade on Exercise Nordic Response 24 in Norway.

AUSTERE CHALLENGE
3 (UK) Div response cell working under V (USA) Corps; and 12 Armoured Brigade Combat Team Force Elements as Lower Control supporting the Estonia 2* HQ.

IMMEDIATE RESPONSE 24
12 Armoured Brigade Combat Team will deploy with two Battlegroups to Poland under 29 Infantry Division (29ID).

COMBINED RESOLVE 24
12 Armoured Brigade Combat Team will Change of Control the Kings Royal Hussars Battlegroups to 3rd Brigade, 101st Airborne Division to conduct combat ready training and validate to Training Level Foxtrot in Grafenwoehr.

SWIFT RESPONSE 24
16 Air Assault Brigade Combat Team, with Aviation components will conduct a Joint Forcible Entry (JFE) into Estonia.

SPRING STORM 24
16 Armoured Brigade Combat Team will take part in the Estonia annual national defence plan Live Exercise with the Estonian Defence Forces (EDF).

The British Army is operating alongside our NATO and JEF allies and partners in Europe. This demonstrates the unity of allies and partners to defending shared values, peace, and security across the continent.

ARMY

a multi-domain demonstration of NATO, national and multinational military capabilities across continental Europe.

"During Steadfast Defender 2024, we coordinated, conducted and sustained complex multi-domain operations over several months, and across thousands of kilometres, from the High North to central and eastern Europe," said Brigadier General Gunnar Bruegner, Supreme Headquarters Allied Powers Europe (SHAPE) the assistant chief of staff responsible for collective training and exercises. "The most important take away is that complex exercises at this scale and ambition remain essential to stress-test our readiness, plans and concepts, and for maintaining our operational coherence and unity."

Britain's role in Steadfast Defender 2024 involved contributing troops to several of the exercises, under the banner of Operation Linotyper. The British units deployed from the bases in Britain by ship, train, and plane. Logistics troops from 104 Theatre Sustainment Brigade deployed first to the British Army base at Sennelager in Germany to receive arriving units. They were then issued with fuel and equipment and sent on their way to Poland, Germany, and the Baltic states.

104 Brigade set up shop at NATO's forward holding base at Normandy Barracks in Sennelager and its 400 strong contingent was code-named Enabling Group South. It comprised 9 Battalion Royal Electrical Mechanical Engineers, 9 Regiment Royal Logistic Corps (RLC), 17 Port and Maritime Regiment, 29 Regiment RLC, 36 Engineer Regiment, 2 Military Intelligence Battalion, 174 Provost Company, 16 Signal Regiment, 1 Medical Regiment and RLC chefs.

LEFT: Senior officers from across NATO watched alliance wargames in Poland in March, 2024. (MOD/CROWN COPYRIGHT)

LEFT: British Paratroopers of 16 Air Assault Brigade travelled to Estonia to take part in Exercise Swift Response in May 2024. (MOD/CROWN COPYRIGHT)

Rapid Reaction

7 Light Mechanised Brigade

ABOVE: Britain's 'Desert Rats' cross the River Vistula in Poland during Exercise Dragon 24 in a major test of allied 'wet gap crossing' skills and capabilities.
(MOD/CROWN COPYRIGHT)

Soldiers from 7 Light Mechanised Brigade Combat Team - the famous Desert Rats – were the first major British combat formation to join Steadfast Defender 2024.

This was aimed at testing the brigade in its role as NATO's Very High Readiness Joint Task Force (Land)(VJTF(L), which has to be ready at 72 hours notice to deploy to any threats to alliance territory.

The 2nd Battalion, Royal Anglian Regiment (2 R ANGLIAN) are the core battlegroup of the brigade, backed up by artillery, engineers, logistics, mechanics, and medics. Other specialist capabilities include drones, air defence, search dogs, and explosive ordinance disposal.

Troops from the Desert Rats flew into Sennelager to join their vehicles which travelled by sea from Marchwood, near Southampton, to Emden in Germany. They then completed a 1,000km road move to the Drawsko Pomorskie Training Area (DPTA) in Poland where they joined Polish troops, as well as those from Albania, Spain, Turkey, and the United States. This was the start of Exercise Dragon 24, which ran from February 28 to March 14. Eventually, 20,000 soldiers and 3,500 military vehicles from nine NATO countries took part in this exercise.

RIGHT: Royal Artillery air defence teams protected 7 Light Mechanised Brigade during Exercise Dragon 24.
(MOD/CROWN COPYRIGHT)

with the German-British Amphibious Engineer Battalion 130 orchestrating the river crossing.

Watching the display from the bank of the eastern shore, Brigadier Guy Foden, commander of 7 Brigade commented: "It's the first time for many in the brigade that they've done a really wide crossing of a major waterway, certainly a river of this width – one of the major waterways in Europe. And we're putting deliberately every element across. So, this is not just a thing for infantry battalions. 6 Regiment RLC will be coming across later, 4 Regiment RA will be bringing their 105mm Light Guns across, Brigade main headquarters is coming across – the whole thing is coming across. But the key thing is, if you use the doctrine, it works."

The unique German-British unit operates 27 M3 Amphibious Bridging Vehicles, known as M3 Rigs, which can operate as individual ferries or be linked together to form a bridge. The unit includes 23 Amphibious Engineer Squadron RE and is the only unit in NATO to have this particular wide, wet, gap-crossing capability.

As soon as this phase was completed, the 2 RANGLIAN battlegroup then deployed once more and completed another road move to eastern Poland. The unit redeployed to Bemowo Piskie Training Area, close to the Suwałki Gap, near the Russian enclave of Kaliningrad. On this part of the exercise, C 'Northamptonshire' and D 'Bedfordshire and Hertfordshire' companies conducted live fire tactical training. Concurrent to this, A 'Lincolnshire' and B 'Leicestershire' companies conducted fighting in built up areas and woodland warfare training areas.

LEFT: Infantry from the Royal Anglian Regiment honed their woodland warfare skills. (MOD/CROWN COPYRIGHT)

It began with 2 R ANGLIAN conducting low level training, working all the way up to a full battlegroup attack. This saw B 'Leicestershire' Company working with the Albanian troops to attack a position in front of various media outlets from across the globe. The battlegroup concluded this with an advance to contact with the Polish and Spanish tank battalions in support.

After this phase of the deployment, the battlegroup then moved to Grupa to conduct a river crossing demonstration across the Vistula River. This saw the unit once again work with NATO allies.

As dawn broke on Wednesday, March 7, a small section of Poland's Vistula River came alive. British, German, Polish, and French military engineers swarmed the western bank, deploying their amphibious rigs in anticipation of the advancing vehicles. Troops of 7 Brigade set up defensive positions around the crossing points.

Eight hours later, the eight ferries had successfully carried more than

750 pieces of equipment and upwards of a thousand troops across the 300m-wide gap, in an impressive display of NATO capability.

The wide wet gap crossing came midway through Exercise Dragon 24,

BELOW: Foxhound armoured vehicles moved 7 Light Mechanised Brigade over hundreds of kilometres during the course of Exercise Dragon 24. (MOD/CROWN COPYRIGHT)

Armoured Fist

12 Armoured Brigade

RIGHT: Challenger 2 main battle tanks of the Kings Royal Hussars and Royal Tank Regiment spearheaded 12 Armoured Brigade's deployment to Europe in May 2024.
(MOD/CROWN COPYRIGHT)

Next to head to Europe were the Challenger 2 main battle tanks of the 12 Armoured Brigade Combat Team. The brigade's move to Europe was a complex logistic exercise, involving the movement of its component units by various means to the British Army's forward holding base at Sennelager.

Many of the units flew to Germany to collect vehicles and equipment from a fleet storage in Sennelager. Other units moved by train through the Channel Tunnel or were loaded on the Ministry of Defence's Point-class roll-on, roll-off ferries.

The brigade was divided into two main groups during Steadfast Defender 2024, with the bulk joining Exercise Immediate Response in April and May in Poland. At the same time, the King's Royal Hussars (KRH) battlegroup moved to the US Joint Multinational Readiness Center near Hohenfels in Bavaria for Exercise Combined Resolve.

In total, the Bulford-based 12 Armoured Brigade deployed nearly

BELOW: A Warrior infantry fighting vehicle of the Royal Welsh Regiment crossing a US Army pontoon bridge during Exercise Immediate Response.
(MOD/CROWN COPYRIGHT)

2,500 personnel and over 800 vehicles to Europe for its exercises. The main group, under the command of 12 Brigade's headquarters, mustered at the vast Drawsko Pomorskie training area near the Polish city of Szczecin. It comprised two battlegroups formed the 1st Battalion, Mercian Regiment (1 MERCIAN) and 1st Battalion, Royal Welsh. Both battlegroups had companies of armoured infantry equipped with Warrior vehicles and squadrons of Challengers from the Royal Tank Regiment.

The brigade's commander, Brigadier Henry Searby, said the exercise was an invaluable training opportunity. "From the moment our first Challenger 2 tank rolled onto a train at Folkestone en route to Poland, we have been testing ourselves and learning hard," he said. "Projecting a force of thousands of people and hundreds of vehicles across Europe into NATO's eastern flank is a substantial challenge. The process has run smoothly, we've integrated with our allies and are running highly effective training missions day and night."

The first week of the exercise was spent in the field conducting lower-level training and learning to work with unmanned aerial vehicles, or UAVs, for short and military working dogs, then attacking positions with a combination of tanks and armoured infantry.

Then troops prepared to move armour and infantry across a body of water, or a 'wide wet gap', using British and American amphibious vehicles and bridges. Once the two armies' engineers had built bridges and set up ferries, tanks, and vehicles from each of the armies moved across.

Lieutenant Colonel Grant Brown, Commanding Officer of 1 MERCIAN, said: "One of the main objectives is interoperability with our NATO allies and we will be working closely with American and Polish troops as the exercise continues. We really don't get much opportunity to exercise with other nations on this scale very often, so to do this delivers an awful lot of combat power. The benefits are learning how other nations operate, what their capabilities are.

"What we are doing here in Poland is one part of a broader exercise across Europe," said Colonel Brown. "We need to be able to display that we are ready because this is a dangerous world and when things happen, they happen very quickly. What we are doing here will have a lasting and reverberating impact."

At the Hohenfels training area, the KRH battlegroup was placed under the command of the US 101st Airborne Division's 3rd Brigade. Exercise Combined Resolve involved 4,000 soldiers from Albania, Bosnia & Herzegovina, Bulgaria, Czech Republic, France, Italy, Lithuania, North Macedonia, Romania, and Slovenia.

ABOVE: The Royal Tank Regiment's Challenger 2s had to operate in dense Polish forests during Exercise Immediate Response.
(MOD/CROWN COPYRIGHT)

LEFT: Royal Logistic Corps experts keep 12 Armoured Brigade's tanks and vehicles fuelled during Exercise Immediate Response.
(MOD/CROWN COPYRIGHT)

Swift Response

16 Air Assault Brigade

RIGHT: Paratroops of 16 Air Assault Brigade operated with air support from Wildcat helicopters during Exercise Swift Response in Estonia.
(MOD/CROWN COPYRIGHT)

Estonia was the venue for the British Army's next Steadfast Defender 2024 linked training event, Exercise Swift Response. This saw 2,300 soldiers and aviators from the British Army's Global Response Force - 16 Air Assault Brigade Combat Team – arriving by air and land to join the action.

Starting from its home at Merville Barracks in Colchester, some 300 vehicles – from police cars to fuel tankers - set off for the 1,500-mile drive to Estonia. The journey took seven days, passing through six overnight camps set up in five different countries. A further 200 vehicles were moved by rail, crossing the English Channel by ferry to be loaded on to trains at Calais.

BELOW: Exercise Swift Response involved a major live firing phase to allow all of 16 Air Assault Brigade's troops to test their weapons in realistic conditions.
(MOD/CROWN COPYRIGHT)

The exercise was aimed at practising rapid entry into operational theatres and started with the Pathfinders, 16 Brigade's advance force, entering Estonia discreetly to find locations for 3rd Battalion, Parachute Regiment battlegroup to arrive by parachute and helicopter.

Some 140 British and US paratroopers jumped from US Air Force Boeing C-17 Globemaster transport aircraft on to a drop zone at Nurmsi marked by Pathfinders. Kiltsi airfield was captured by British and Polish paratroopers in an air assault operation, supported by Boeing AH-64E Apache attack, Leonardo Wildcat reconnaissance, and Boeing Chinook HC5/6 support helicopters of 4 Regiment Army Air Corps battlegroup.

After Kiltsi was secured, the paratroopers were lifted from Nurmsi by Chinooks, while a specialist airfield damage repair team from 23 Parachute Engineer Regiment RE brought the runway into operation. Over the next 24 hours, further

troops, equipment, and vehicles arrived at Kiltsi by US Boeing C-17s Globemasters and RAF Airbus A400M Atlas transport aircraft. Then 1st Battalion, Royal Irish Regiment, pushed out into the surrounding countryside in Jackal and Foxhound patrol vehicles to grow a security bubble around the airfield.

The culmination of the exercise was the delivery of a Multiple Launch Rocket System (MLRS) in an A400M. The powerful artillery system – dubbed 'the 70km sniper' – carried out a simulated fire mission to strike targets allowing the force to make its next move.

Brigadier Mark Berry, commander of 16 Brigade, said: "16 Air Assault Brigade Combat Team is uniquely ready - for any operation, any task, anywhere in the world. Putting soldiers into battle by air is an immensely complex and demanding activity, »

ABOVE: British Paratroopers carried out a live firing exercise in trenches during Exercise Swift Response to test their ability to defend fortified positions.
(MOD/CROWN COPYRIGHT)

LEFT: Army Air Corps AH-64E Apache attack helicopters flew to Estonia in May 2024 for their first major NATO exercise.
(MOD/CROWN COPYRIGHT)

BELOW: A Royal Army MLRS launcher was airlifted in a RAF A400M Atlas during Exercise Swift Response to demonstrate that the power weapon could be easily moved by air.
(MOD/CROWN COPYRIGHT)

for which 16 Brigade trains hard. Our work in Estonia has developed our specialist skills alongside our allies and demonstrated both our capability and our readiness to rapidly project force in support of our NATO allies."

After Swift Response wrapped up, 16 Brigade moved to take part in a wider test of NATO's plans to defend Estonia. Exercise Spring Storm 2024 saw the Estonia national defence plan being tested to counter a simulated Russian invasion from the east. British troops from the NATO Enhanced Forward Battlegroup brought their Challenger 2 tanks and Warrior armoured vehicles into the fray to support Estonian infantry units. This practised mobile defence, with columns of tanks and armour moving to reinforce infantry positions. The Apache helicopters of 16 Brigade flew to support the defending troops.

Helping Ukraine

Bring up the Big Guns

All of the British Army's AS90 155mm self-propelled are to be retired in nine months time and handed over to the Ukrainian military. The first stage of the retirement process occurred in May, 2024 when 1 Regiment Royal Horse Artillery (1RHA) fired its last live rounds in the UK on Salisbury Plain.

According to the regiment's social media posts, after its last battery completes a nine-month operational tour in Estonia, the remaining six guns will be retired.

"After 30 years of distinguished service we do not quite yet say farewell to the much loved, battle-proven self-propelled guns," said the regiment. "The Chestnut Troop (Ed: actually, a battery sized sub-unit) will operate the system for the next nine months in Estonia."

The plan is to hand over the Royal Artillery's remaining fleet of less than 30 guns, as well as the remaining spare stockpile to the Ukrainians. "They need them more than we do so we will have to take this on the chin," said the source.

The Royal Artillery is currently bringing its interim buy of 14 Archer 155mm guns into service and it will have to make do with them for close fire support until the first Remote-Controlled Howitzer 155mm (RCH 155) 52 calibre Wheeled Artillery Systems come online later in the decade.

Between 1992 and 1995 the Royal Artillery took delivery of 179 AS90s from the then Vickers Shipbuilding and Engineering company (VSEL) at Barrow-in-Furness, but a series of defence cuts left it with only 89 in service at the start of this decade, divided between 1 RHA and 19 Regiment RA. Prime Minister Rishi Sunak gave a first batch of AS90s to Ukraine last year and by April the UK had gifted 50 to Kyiv.

Royal Artillery officers say the AS90 fleet has been plagued by serviceability issues recently because of a finite pool of spares and they doubted it would have reached the previously projected 2032 out of service date. "Giving the guns to Ukraine makes sense but it leaves us short in the near term," said one Royal Artillery officer.

LEFT: All of the Royal Artillery's remaining AS90 155mm guns will have been transferred to the Ukrainian army by early 2025. (MOD/CROWN COPYRIGHT)

LEFT: More than 30,000 Ukrainian soldiers have been trained by the British Army since June 2022. (MOD/CROWN COPYRIGHT)

BELOW: The Royal Artillery began training Ukraine gunners to fire the AS90 at the start of 2023. (MOD/CROWN COPYRIGHT)

In Action in the Middle East

Air Defence and Air Drops

RIGHT: Royal Logistic Corps air dispatchers have played an import role in the operation to air drop humanitarian aid to Gaza. (MOD/CROWN COPYRIGHT)

BELOW: High Value Missile (HVM) teams from 12 Regiment RA have been on duty in Iraq since early 2023. (MOD/CROWN COPYRIGHT)

After Hamas fighters invaded Israel on October 7, 2023, the British Army found itself in the firing line as the conflict spread across the Middle East.

This eventually resulted in the Royal Artillery shooting down an Iranian-made kamikaze drone in the Middle East, in the first kill

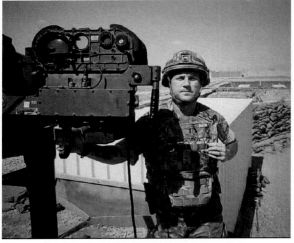

of an enemy aircraft in combat by the British Army since the 1982 Falklands war.

The British Army has had detachments of troops deployed across Iraq and Syria as part of the US-led mission to defeat the so-called Islamic State (ISIS) since 2015. In

2022 they had started to come under attack from pro-Iranian militia groups opposed to the coalition presence in the Middle East. This prompted a call going out to the Royal Artillery to dispatch Thales Starstreak High Velocity Missile (HVM) detachments to join Operation Shader. These were

ABOVE: Royal Artillery air defenders shot down an Iranian-made drone in Iraq in December 2023. (MOD/CROWN COPYRIGHT)

equipped with the man portable Light Weight Launchers and were positioned around British bases, including the main logistic base at Erbil airport in northern Iraq.

The one-way-attack drone was shot down in December 2023 during an attack on Al Assad airbase in western Iraq by Gunners of 170 (Imjin) Battery Royal Artillery, using the HVM.

The detachment of 170 Battery redeployed to the US-controlled Al Assad airbase last October after Iranian-backed militia groups started launching drone and rocket attacks on coalition bases in Iraq and Syria in response to the Gaza war. "The Americans had a gap in their air defence capabilities, so we dispatched an HVM team from our base at Erbil airport," said the military source. "A force protection team from the Royal Yorkshire Regiment went with them."

HVMs supplied to Ukraine in 2022 have scored several kills against Russian aircraft, helicopters, and drones but December 2023 is the first time a British Army ground-based air defence weapon has been used in anger since the Falklands. Early model Rapier and Blowpipe missiles were deployed to protect the British bridgehead at San Carlos Water from Argentine air attack in 1982.

In March 2024, Royal Air Force Airbus A400M Atlas airlifters started to drop humanitarian aid to starving civilians in Gaza, as part of joint operations with the US and Jordanian air forces. Air dispatchers from the Royal Logistic Corps are an integral part of the crews of RAF airlifts during parachute dropping missions. So, a contingent of 47 Air Dispatch Squadron RLC went with the RAF to King Abdullah II Air Base near Amman in Jordan to begin preparing pallets of aid for air dropping. The air dispatchers then flew on the missions, pushing the cargo pallets off the rear ramps of the A400Ms.

ABOVE: RAF A400M Atlas airlifters began dropping humanitarian aid into war ravaged Gaza in March 2024. (MOD/CROWN COPYRIGHT)

LEFT: 47 Air Dispatch Squadron RLC traces it history back to World War Two and remains the British armed forces subject matter expert for the aerial delivery of troops and cargo. (MOD/CROWN COPYRIGHT)

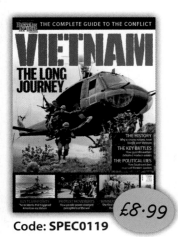
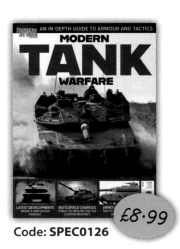

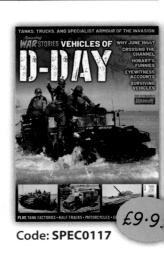
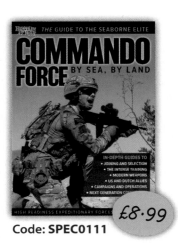

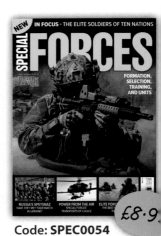

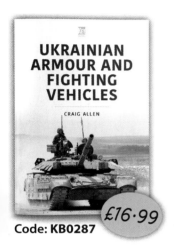
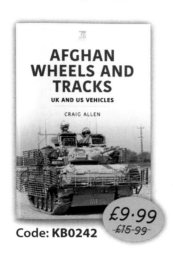
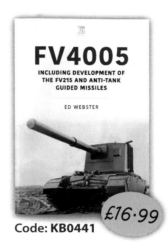
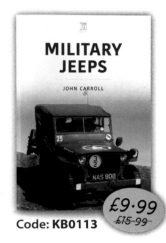
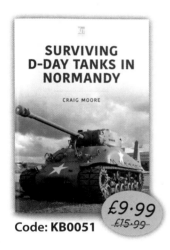

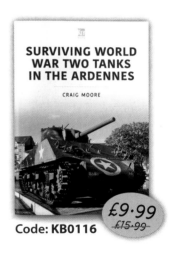

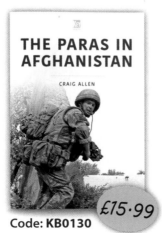
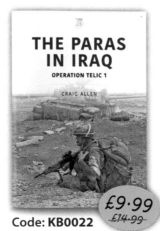
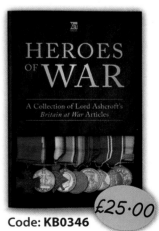

D-Day

The Longest Day

British Army veterans gathered in Normandy this June, 80 years on from D-Day, to commemorate the Allied amphibious and airborne operation that opened the way for the defeat of German forces in France.

The British Army had a major role in D-Day, with 7,900 airborne troops landing in Normandy in the early hours of June 6. Hours later the 3rd and 50th Infantry Divisions stormed ashore on Sword and Gold Beach, respectively.

Britain's General Bernard Montgomery, or Monty as he was known, was the overland commander of the allied land forces on D-Day and he ensured that meticulous planning and preparation took place ahead of the landings.

So, when the invasion armada set sail for Normandy on the evening of June 5, confidence was high that within hours the Allied troops would be securely ashore on mainland Europe.

The first British troops to land were airborne pathfinders who parachuted into Normandy to mark drop zones for the troops of the 6th Airborne Division. The

first objective to be captured by the strategic bridges over the Caen Canal and Orne River, which was seized by glider landed troops of the Oxford & Buckinghamshire Light Infantry.

As the first landing craft hit Gold and Sword beaches just after dawn,

they met fierce resistance from the German machine gun nests and artillery that had not been fully neutralised by naval gunfire and bomber strikes. Hundreds of soldiers were killed or wounded by German fire, but the British assault did not get

bogged down in the same way as the Americans landing on Omaha Beach to the west.

To blast through the fortifications of Hitler's Atlantic Wall, the British Army had developed specialist tanks to lead in the invasion and they showed their worth on D-Day. Swimming Duplex Drive (DD) tanks hit the beaches ahead of the landing craft carrying the main infantry assault force, to silence German gun emplacements. Engineering tanks carrying bulldozers and fascines to fill anti-tank ditches came ashore next to clear a path off the beaches. The last German resistance was neutralised by flame thrower Crocodile tanks and naval gunfire.

Within hours of landing, the first British columns were heading inland to link up with the airborne forces. By early in the afternoon of June 6, commandos from Sword Beach had linked up with the defenders of the Bénouville Bridge, which was soon renamed Pegasus Bridge in honour of the British Airborne Forces.

After a day of heavy fighting, British forces were firmly established in Normandy, but a heavy price had been paid. Out of the 24,970 British troops who landed on Gold Beach there were 1,100 casualties, of which 350 were killed. On Sword Beach, 683 British soldiers were killed out of 28,845 who landed. The 6th Airborne Division suffered 800 casualties, including 300 dead.

Despite the success of the Allied landings, the German army was not yet defeated. For the next three months, the Germans put up fanatical resistance and only started to retreat after overwhelming numbers of Allied troops joined the advance, backed by massive Allied air power. By August, German resistance had been broken and the Nazi army was in full retreat back to the Rhine.

D-Day was a true turning point in World War Two, and the surviving veterans who travelled to Normandy this June, were rightly lauded as heroes.

Battle for Radfan

Retreat from Empire

RIGHT: British troops were dependent on RAF Belvedere helicopters to move supplies up into the rugged Radfan mountains.
(IMPERIAL WAR MUSEUM)

Sixty years ago, Britain still controlled large swathes of the Middle East and Africa, but the 'winds of change' were signalling the imminent end of the British Empire.

In 1964, the country we now know as Yemen was British ruled South Arabia. British forces were concentrated in the city of Aden, where a strategic airbase and port were located. The British ran South Arabia through a network of tribal alliances, but its grip on

RIGHT: Paratroops spearheaded the British advance into Radfan in April 1964.
(IMPERIAL WAR MUSEUM)

the territory was being rocked by Arab nationalists who wanted to drive out their imperial overseers. In December 1963, a hand grenade was thrown at the British governor in Aden's airport. To try to clamp down on unrest, the British declared a state of emergency and military reinforcements rushed to the country to bolster security.

By April 1964, the British were convinced the rebels in Aden City

RIGHT: Rebel tribesmen put up fierce resistance to the British advance into Radfan.
(IMPERIAL WAR MUSEUM)

were being armed and supplied from the mountainous Radfan region. This desolate region was controlled by heavily armed tribesmen, who had thrown their lot in with the nationalist rebels.

A military expedition to Radfan was ordered to disrupt rebel supply lines, led 3rd Battalion, The Parachute Regiment (3 PARA) and Royal Marines of 45 Commando, back up 105mm pack howitzers from the 7th Regiment Royal Horse Artillery (RHA) and locally recruited South Arabian army soldiers.

The mountainous terrain and baking hot climate made the Radfan one of the most demanding environments the British Army had ever fought in. There were few roads in the region, so the British force was dependent on air supply keep fighting, particularly delivering water to forward positions.

The RAF set up a forward air strip at Thumeir to allow Beverly transport aircraft to land troops and supplies. Twin-rotor Belvedere heavy helicopters carried supplies and the RHA's guns to forward positions. This was the first time the British Army

had relied on helicopters for a major operation.

Radforce, as the British group was nicknamed, was given the objective of seizing and then searching the mountainous strongholds of a pro-rebel tribe, who were ominously nicknamed the Red Wolves.

The attack was supposed to begin with a parachute landing by 3 PARA into the enemy heartland. A patrol of the Special Air Service (SAS) was ordered to infiltrate the enemy stronghold and mark the drop zone for 3 PARA. However, the SAS men were soon discovered and came under attack by the rebels, only keeping the enemy at bay thanks to air strikes by RAF Hawker Hunter jets, but the fighting left two SAS men dead. The rebels later decapitated their bodies. The surviving SAS men only escaped under cover of darkness.

The setback led to Radforce having to march into battle, but after a brutal march over the mountains, 3 PARA and Royal Marines assaulted the enemy stronghold and drove out the Red Wolves. After nearly a month of heavy fighting, 3 PARA withdrew to Aden having won a Distinguished Service Order, a Military Cross, and four additional medals, three Mentioned in Dispatches and six Commander in Chief's commendations.

The rebels melted away into the mountains and at first the British were convinced they had dealt their enemy a heavy blow. However, the respite did not last long. Over the next three years South Arabia was engulfed in fighting. During the Aden Emergency 92 British military personnel were killed and 500 wounded.

In 1967, the British government decided to call it a day, and withdrew the last troops from Aden. The British Empire's days were now, well, and truly, numbered.

ABOVE: Royal Marines joined Paratroopers as part of Radforce in April 1964. (IMPERIAL WAR MUSEUM)

LEFT: 105mm Pack Howitzers of 7th Regiment Royal Horse Artillery provided fire support for Radforce. (IMPERIAL WAR MUSEUM)

Kosovo

British Army Leads NATO Peacekeeping Force

ABOVE: Vital bridges and tunnels in the strategic Kaçanik Gorge were secured by 5 Airborne Brigade to open the way for KFOR to enter Kosovo.
(MOD/CROWN COPYRIGHT)

In 1999, the Yugoslav province of Kosovo was the centre of a major international conflict as its majority Albanian population clashed with Serbian security forces. International diplomats tried to mediate between the Albanians and Yugoslav president Slobodan Milosevic but when a peace conference in France failed, the US and its NATO allies issued an ultimatum for the withdrawal of Serbian troops and police from Kosovo.

RIGHT: RAF Chinook helicopters moved Paratroopers to the outskirts of Pristina as NATO peacekeeping forces closed in on the capital of Kosovo.
(MOD/CROWN COPYRIGHT)

The British Army played an important part in the international response to the crisis, deploying its first troops to neighbouring Macedonia in December 1999 as tension escalated. Soldiers from the King's Own Royal Border Regiment were assigned to a NATO rapid reaction force that was ready to evacuate international observers sent to try to mediate between the warring sides in Kosovo.

They were soon joined by the British-led Allied Rapid Reaction Corps Headquarters, under the command of Lieutenant General Mike Jackson, and troops from 4 Armoured Brigade. General Jackson was supposed to be preparing to lead a peacekeeping force into Kosovo to supervise any peace agreement. Within days of NATO starting its bombing campaign on March 24, General Jackson's troops started to provide humanitarian aid to the hundreds of thousands of Albanian refugees fleeing over the border into Macedonia.

By the evening, British troops were in control of Pristina and Serb troops were crossing out of Kosovo. While 5 Brigade remained in Pristina to secure the city, the tanks of 4 Brigade headed north to secure the border with Serbia. Within days, General Jackson had moved his headquarters to the outskirts of Pristina to oversee the return of Albanian refugees and the establishment of a United Nations-led civilian administration.

British troops entered Kosovo without firing a shot. They were greeted as liberators by cheering crowds as they marched into Pristina. Kosovo had been devastated by months of conflict. British troops were soon involved in re-establishing public utilities, repairing bridges and buildings, establishing schools, and helping set up medical services. A big job was to fill the vacuum until a UN civilian police force was in place to maintain law and order.

Twenty five years later, Kosovo is peaceful and prosperous. The country has declared itself independent, but KFOR remains on duty to secure the international agreements that led to the withdrawal of Serb troops. Britain continues to contribute small numbers of troops to KFOR and reinforcements from the Princess of Wales Royal Regiment were sent to Kosovo last October when tension with Serbia escalated, but this soon eased. Britain remains popular with Kosovo's Albanian population. A statue has even been unveiled in the centre of Pristina to British Prime Minister Tony Blair to honour his role in the 1999 conflict.

LEFT: The Kosovo insertion mission was the British Army's largest ever air mobile operation. (MOD/CROWN COPYRIGHT)

BELOW: Paratroopers soon set about restoring law and order in Pristina ahead of the arrival of a civilian UN police force. (MOD/CROWN COPYRIGHT)

By late May, Milosevic could see the game was up and agreed to withdraw his troops. General Jackson started to negotiate with the Yugoslav military for peacekeepers from NATO's Kosovo Force (KFOR) to take over from them. To reinforce the KFOR, the British 5 Airborne Brigade was flown out to Macedonia.

When the Serbian troops started leaving on June 12, 5 Brigade spearheaded the move of KFOR into Kosovo. Landing by helicopter in the Kaçanik Gorge to secure the main road from Macedonia to Pristina, the capital of the province. Once the key bridges and tunnels were declared clear, the tanks of 4 Brigade started to roll forward towards Pristina. Royal Air Force Chinook helicopters then delivered the 1st Battalion, Parachute Regiment to landing zones outside the city to begin its liberation.

British Army in 2024

Ready to Fight

ABOVE: In 2023, soldiers from the Scots Guards took part in exercises in South Korea. (MOD/CROWN COPYRIGHT)

In 2021, an ambitious programme was launched to reorganise and reform the British Army. The final phases of the Future Soldier project are now slotting into place, and almost all of the unit reorganisations are complete.

At the beginning of April 2024, the British Army had 72,510 trained regular soldiers and 24,070 trained army reservists. This was below the 2021 Future Soldier plan's personnel target of 73,000 regular soldiers that was to have been reached by 2025.

Over the next three to four years, the re-equipment programme will gather momentum with new tanks, armoured vehicles, and artillery being rolled out. A programme of tactical experimentation has already begun to work out how to use this new equipment to best effect.

The British Army of 2024 is built around two core formations. Its heavy armoured, or war fighting division, is 3 (UK) Division and 1 (UK) Division is configured to lead expeditionary operations outside of Europe.

To support these formations, there are several enabling brigades or groups which provide aviation, engineering, logistic,

communications, information, and other specialist capabilities.

Britain continues to play a leading role in NATO and provides a three-star

RIGHT: All roles in the British Army are now open to female soldiers. (MOD/CROWN COPYRIGHT)

moved garrison every two or three years. Now British brigades, regiments and battalions have fixed garrisons.

This does not mean the British Army has turned into 'home birds'. Operational deployments and exercises mean British soldiers are now routinely away from their garrisons for several months a year. Operational rotations in Eastern Europe, the Middle East and the Falklands involve thousands of soldiers each year. Training exercises in Europe, the Middle East, Africa, Belize, Kenya, Brunei, and the Far East involve even more troops. And two battalions remain in Cyprus in the last overseas posting where infantry soldiers can live with their families.

While expeditionary operations overseas are the core business of the British Army, it still has important roles to play at home. Government ministries, devolved administrations and local councils can call on the British Army in time of emergency. Military Aid to Civil Authority, or MACA, missions see soldiers building flood defences, putting out forest fires, or working in airports during strikes by Border Force staff. The largest ever MACA operation was launched during the COVID-19 pandemic when tens of thousands of military personnel were deployed to keep essential services operational and assist the National Health Service.

The British Army is very different from when it fought the Iraq and Afghan wars earlier this century. It is now ready to fight in Europe and operate further afield.

LEFT: New rockets are being purchased to enhance the firepower of the Royal Artillery's MLRS. (MOD/CROWN COPYRIGHT)

BELOW: A major re-equipment programme is underway for the British Army. In January 2024, the new Ajax reconnaissance vehicles underwent cold weather trials in the north of Sweden. (MOD/CROWN COPYRIGHT)

headquarters known as the Allied Rapid Reaction Corps (ARRC), under the command of a lieutenant general to the alliance and it is configured to lead a hard-hitting reserve force in time of crisis or war in Europe.

Over the past decade the British Army has moved almost all of its brigades and regiments back to Britain from Germany. At the same time, it has ended what used to be known as the 'Arms Plot' where each regiment

How the British Army is Organised

Set to Fight

RIGHT: The Royal Logistic Corps has the job of moving the British Army around the world for training and operations.
(MOD/CROWN COPYRIGHT)

BELOW: More than 16,000 British troops were deployed to Europe in the first half of 2024 for NATO's Exercise Steadfast Defender.
(MOD/CROWN COPYRIGHT)

The British Army sets great store on the historical traditions of its famous regiments and their iconic titles. It is, however, a modern fighting force and once in the field it is organised very differently from back in its home barracks.

In peacetime, most soldiers are organised into regiments or battalions. An infantry regiment comprises one or more battalions, which each have around three or four companies of between 120 to 150 soldiers. A company is in turn made up of three or four platoons with some 30 soldiers. Each platoon in turn usually comprises three eight-soldier-strong sections and a small command team. The Royal Armoured Corps and other branches

and arms of service, such as the Royal Engineers, Royal Logistic Corps, and Army Air Corps call their company-sized units squadrons. The Royal Artillery calls its company-sized units batteries. Their platoons are called troops, except in the AAC, where they are called flights. An armoured troop usually has four tanks, and four troops make up a squadron. Battalions are usually commanded by a lieutenant colonel, company-sized units are led by majors, and platoons are commanded by lieutenants or captains.

Once activated for exercises or operations, infantry battalions or regiments of other combat arms are called battlegroups because they normally have specialist units from other arms attached. So, an infantry battalion could have a squadron of tanks or battery of guns, attached for a specific mission to create a battlegroup. The term was adopted because of the way the German army successfully used the concept in World War Two. The US Army uses the term Task Force to describe a combined-arms, battalion-sized, unit and the British Army is starting to use the designation for units assigned to work under US command.

The next highest level of command is a brigade. These are used for operations involving multiple battlegroups. In the 2021 defence review it was announced that they would now be known as brigade combat teams, which is the American term. Brigades are also referred to as one-star headquarters and are led by a brigadier.

When mobilised for operations and major exercises, divisional and brigade headquarters can take under command a mix of units and capabilities. The armoured infantry brigades comprise three or four battlegroups, backed up by supporting formation reconnaissance, close support artillery, medical evacuation, logistic, surveillance, and aviation support units. The brigade commander is the highest-ranking officer who would lead troops into action, with brigadiers in the 1991 and 2003 Gulf Wars directing operations from the turret of a tank to allow them to view events unfolding in real time.

Since 1990, the British Army has generally used its brigades as the building block for overseas deployments and then adding specialist units before brigades go into the field. Every brigade took

their turn to deploy to the Balkans, Iraq, and Afghanistan in a series of back-to-back rotations, or roulements.

Multiple brigades are commanded by a divisional, or two-star headquarters, with a major general in command. Higher level operations are controlled by three-star, or corps-level headquarters. The British Army only has one such headquarters, the NATO-assigned Allied Rapid Reaction Corps (ARRC).

After the British Army returned all its troops from Germany between 2010 and 2019, it effectively stopped the process of moving units around between garrisons, except for the two infantry battalions on Cyprus. This exercise, known as the 'Arms Plot', saw most regiments and battalions moved between garrisons every two to three years to give troops and their families a chance to live overseas. However, it cost huge amounts of money. Now, units do not move around, and individuals are moved between units on promotion. This limits disruptions to soldiers' families but means the idea of soldiers serving their entire careers within one unit to build cohesion and esprit de corps is a thing of the past.

Specialist Regiments and Corps of British Army
Adjutant General's Corps: AGC
Army Air Corps: AAC
Corps of Royal Electrical & Mechanical Engineers: REME
Corps of Royal Engineers: RE
Intelligence Corps: IC
Queen Alexandra's Royal Army Nursing Corps: QARNC
Royal Armoured Corps: RAC
Royal Army Dental Corps: RADC
Royal Army Medical Corps: RAMC
Royal Army Veterinary Corps: RAVC
Royal Logistic Corps: RLC
Royal Military Police: RMP
Royal Regiment of Artillery: RA
Special Air Service Regiment: SAS

LEFT: Infantry soldiers remain the core of the British Army's fighting power.
(MOD/CROWN COPYRIGHT)

LEFT: The Royal Engineers deployed M3 bridging rigs to Poland for Exercise Dragon 24 to enable the British Army to cross the mighty River Vistula.
(MOD/CROWN COPYRIGHT)

3 (UK) Division

The Iron Division

The British Army's heavy armoured forces are concentrated into the Bulford-based 3 (United Kingdom) Division. It is trained and equipped to fight what are termed 'near peer' opponents. In other words, enemy armoured forces in high intensity combat. Today, this means the Russian army.

It controls the three Challenger 2 main battle tank equipped regiments of the Royal Armour Corps and four Warrior fighting vehicle equipped armoured infantry battalions. The Royal Artillery's Multiple Launch Rocket Systems (MLRS) long range attack weapons are the division's main strike power, along with any Boeing AH-64E Apache attack helicopters that might be attached.

The division can trace its history back to the time of the Duke of Wellington and Napoleon, but it was in World War Two that it established its reputation as one of the British Army's most professional fighting formations. Under the command

of the then Major General Bernard Montgomery, it formed the rear guard during the 1940 retreat to Dunkirk. Monty, famously, brought home almost all of his troops from France and the then 3rd Infantry Division was earmarked to spearhead the invasion of Europe. It landed on Sword Beach on D-Day and successfully linked up with the British Airborne troops holding Pegasus Bridge.

During the post-war period, the division served in the British Army of the Rhine (BAOR) as an armoured formation. It returned to Britain in the 1990s and was reformed as 3 (UK) Mechanised Division. In 1996 it spearheaded NATO's peacekeeping mission in Bosnia and then in the summer of 2003 led the British occupation force in the southern Iraqi city of Basra.

Since the Future Soldier plan was announced in 2021 and the Operation Mobilise initiative in 2023, the division has been re-organised to enable it to rapidly deploy to Eastern Europe to reinforce NATO allies. The division has been providing the British armoured battlegroup in Estonia since 2017 and in 2022 this commitment was increased to reinforcing the Baltic state with a full brigade if it should be threatened with attack. One of the division's brigades is designed as the Forward Land Force (FLF) brigade and has to be ready to deploy en mass to the Baltic region.

A pool of pre-positioned equipment has been established at the old British garrison in Sennelager in Germany, holding enough vehicles and equipment for two battalion-sized battlegroups for the FLF brigade. In time of crisis, the personnel would be flown out to Germany to activate this equipment and then moved by train to Eastern Europe to join NATO allies.

3 (UK) Division	
Headquarters	Picton Barracks, Bulford Camp
7 Signals Group	**Bulford Camp**
Headquarters	
1 Signals Regiment	Swinton Barracks, Pernham Down
3 Signals Regiment	Bulford Barracks, Bulford
15 Signals Regiment	Swinton Barracks, Pernham Down
71 Signals Regiment (Army Reserve)	Bexley Heath
Information Manoeuvre Units	
4 Military Intelligence Battalion, IC	Kiwi Barracks, Bulford
7 Military Intelligence Battalion, IC	Bristol
1 Military Police Brigade	Andover
1 Regiment RMP	Catterick
3 Regiment RMP	Bulford
Special Investigation Branch	Bulford
Special Operations Unit	Southwick Park
Military Provost Staff Corps	Colchester

In 2023 and 2024, these procedures have been put to the test by 3 (UK) Division's units.

The division is already in the process of receiving the first batches of new weapons and armoured vehicles. Its artillery regiments are already bringing the new Archer 155mm self-propelled guns into service. Next year it will start to receive the first of its new Boxer wheeled armoured personnel carriers and possibly the first production standard Ajax armoured reconnaissance vehicles.

In 2027, the first upgraded Challenger 3 main battle tanks should start to arrive.

LEFT: Planners in 3 (UK) Division headquarters have the job of massing the formation's impressive firepower for decisive effect. (MOD/CROWN COPYRIGHT)

BELOW: All of 3 (UK) Division's tanks, armoured vehicles, and artillery are scheduled to be replaced with new equipment over the coming decade. (MOD/CROWN COPYRIGHT)

12 Armoured Brigade

Ace of Spades

RIGHT: Brigadier Henry Searby is the current commander of 12 Armoured Brigade.
(MOD/CROWN COPYRIGHT)

The formation is one of two armoured brigade combat teams (BCT) in 3 (UK) Division. According to the Future Soldier plan, the BCT are meant to be a self-containing fighting force, bringing together main battle tanks, mechanised infantry, reconnaissance, logistic, medical and repair units into a single formation.

12 Armoured BCT was reformed in 2022 out of the old 12 Armoured Infantry Brigade and it has since been building up its capability to rapidly deploy to Eastern Europe, including playing a leading role in NATO's Exercise Steadfast Defender. Its headquarters is in Bulford garrison and its major units are close-by on Salisbury Plain. Its troops live in a number of 'super garrisons' around Salisbury Plain, which have single living accommodation, or barracks, and vehicle garages close by.

The brigade remains a 'square' formation with two armoured regiments and two armoured infantry battalions, as its core units. This is

a transitional state until the King's Royal Hussars (KRH) trade in their Challenger 2 main battle tanks for Ajax reconnaissance vehicles.

Its armoured fist is provided by the KRH and the Royal Tank Regiment (RTR). They both operate the Challenger 2, and each have four

BELOW: The Royal Tank Regiment is one of 12 Armoured Brigade's two armoured regiments.
(MOD/CROWN COPYRIGHT)

'sabre' squadrons, with 11 tanks. In time of war an additional troop of four tanks would be provided by reserve crews from the Royal Wessex Yeomanry to bring the strength of regiment up to 58 tanks.

When the Ajax family of reconnaissance vehicles is ready to

enter service, it is planned that the KRH will transition to them and become the brigade's reconnaissance unit. Its role will be to scout ahead of the brigade finding enemy forces or acting as a screen to cover terrain during defensive operations.

The Royal Welsh and Mercian Regiments each currently provide the brigade with a battalion of armoured infantry, mounted in Warrior infantry fighting vehicles. These vehicles are supposed to be retired in 2025 and replaced with the Boxer wheeled armoured personnel carrier. This is expected to slip because of delays to the Boxer delivery schedule.

Plans to re-role armoured infantry battalions into mechanised units were announced in the Future Soldier

12 Armoured Brigade Combat Team	
Headquarters & Signals Squadron	Bulford Barracks, Bulford
Armoured Regiment (Challenger 2)	
Royal Tank Regiment	Aliwal Barracks, Tidworth
King's Royal Hussars (to be armoured cavalry 2025)	Aliwal Barracks, Tidworth
Armoured Infantry Battalion (Warrior/Bulldog)	
1st Battalion, Royal Welsh Regiment	Lucknow Barracks, Tidworth
1st Battalion, Mercian Regiment	Picton Lines, Bulford
Light-role Infantry Battalion (Army Reserve)	
3rd Battalion, Royal Welsh Regiment	Cardiff
4th Battalion, Mercian Regiment	Wolverhampton
Logistic Support Group	
2 Medical Regiment RAMC	Tidworth
4 Regiment RLC	Dalton Barracks, Abingdon
4 (Armoured Close Support) Regiment REME	Jellalabad Barracks, Tidworth

plan in 2021 when the project to buy an upgraded version of the Warrior was scrapped on cost grounds. Consequently, the British Army is developing new ways of fighting because the Boxer lacks the firepower, cross country mobility, and armour to deliver infantry soldiers direct onto enemy positions. In future, the Boxer equipped battalions will have operational level mobility, but their infantry soldiers will have to close on the enemy on foot.

In time of war, the brigade will be reinforced by Army Reserve infantry battalions from the Royal Welsh and Mercian Regiments to defend key terrain or provide rear area security.

The brigade is provided with an integral logistic support group to keep it fighting. This is led by »

LEFT: A Warrior infantry fighting vehicle sporting the 'ace of spades' insignia with 12 Armoured Brigade during Exercise Immediate Response in Poland, May 2024. (MOD/CROWN COPYRIGHT)

BELOW: Royal Engineers ferry 12 Armoured Brigade vehicles across a river during Exercise Immediate Response in Poland in May 2024. (MOD/CROWN COPYRIGHT)

ABOVE: Armoured infantry from the Royal Welsh Regiment provides close support for the brigade's Challenger tanks.
(MOD/CROWN COPYRIGHT)

RIGHT: The King's Royal Hussars battlegroup was detached from 12 Armoured Brigade for Exercise Combined Response in Germany in May 2024.
(MOD/CROWN COPYRIGHT)

Challenger 2 Main Battle Tank	
Manufacturer:	Vickers Defence Systems
Unit cost:	£4.2m
Produced:	1993 to 2002
Number built:	447 built, 213 still in use by the British Army in 2024
Specifications	
Mass:	64 tonnes
Length:	8.3m (27ft 3in), 13.5m (44ft 3in)
Width:	3.5m (11ft 6in)
Height:	2.49m (8ft 2in)
Crew:	Four (commander, gunner, loader/operator, driver)
Main armament:	L30A1 120mm rifled gun
Secondary armament:	Coaxial 7.62mm L94A1 chain gun EX-34, 7.62mm L37A2 Operator/Loader's hatch machine gun
Engine:	Perkins CV12-6A V12 diesel
Maximum speed:	59kph (37mph) on road

4 Regiment RLC and also includes 4 Battalion REME and 2 Medical Regiment RAMC. These units allow the brigade to recover and repair any damaged vehicles, as well as evacuating wounded personnel from frontline positions. Several days of supplies and ammunition can be carried in 4 Regiment RLC's trucks to allow frontline units to be resupplied.

All the brigade's major units are trained and configured to allow them to be rapidly regrouped into all arms battlegroups. Currently, the brigade has enough armoured squadrons and infantry companies to form four battle groups. So, the two armoured regiments could each take under command an armoured infantry company. The two armoured infantry battalions could each take under command a tank squadron. All these battle groups have the combat potential to carry out offensive or defensive operations. The tactics needed to launch offensive operations without Warriors are still being developed.

The British Army is working on a new doctrine to provide fire support for its brigades. It is increasing emphasis on the deep battle, hitting targets far behind enemy lines with attack helicopters and rockets. The retirement of the AS90 155mm self-propelled gun means there will be fewer guns available to provide close support to specific infantry or armoured units.

Since 2017, the brigade's regiments and battalions have taken their turn to deploy to Estonia as part of NATO's Enhanced Forward Battlegroup. This provided the brigade with plenty of experience in working with NATO allies.

As part of the build-up for Exercise Steadfast Defender 2024, the brigade's

12 Armoured Brigade History

The brigade traces its history back to 1900 when it was formed during the Boer War, and it was part of the British Expeditionary Force (BEF) that crossed the channel in 1914 to face the Germans in the opening weeks of World War One. It saw hard fighting on the Western Front for the rest of the war.

In World War Two it saw action in France in 1940 and then in the Mediterranean theatre, including in North Africa, Italy, and Greece. It served in the British Army of the Rhine during the Cold War as an armoured formation. The brigade was disbanded in 1992 as part of the peace dividend.

The 1998 Strategic Defence Review resurrected the brigade as part of 3 (UK) Mechanised Division to allow its parent formation to establish a readiness cycle to rotate its three brigades to overseas operations. Over the past 25 years, the brigade took its turn to deploy on six month-long operational tours to Kosovo, Iraq, and Afghanistan.

The brigade saw heavy combat in Afghanistan in 2007, when the Taliban insurgency was at its height. It returned to Afghanistan for a final tour in 2012. After returning from Operation Herrick, it was earmarked to become one of the British Army's two strike brigades, which were supposed to be able to rapidly deploy to crisis zones around Europe. When the strike brigade concept was scrapped in 2021, it was re-designated as an armoured brigade combat team the following year.

battle groups have gone through a year-long training cycle. During 2023 key personnel first took part in synthetic training at the Combined Arms Tactical Trainer (CATT) simulation centre at Sennelager garrison, near Paderborn. Troops then drew armoured vehicles and other equipment from climate-controlled storage hangers at the NATO Forward Holding Base at Sennelager. These vehicles are known as the Land Training Fleet. The units then deployed to the Paderborn training area or other training locations in Germany and Poland. Known as Exercise Iron Storm, these training events often involved units of the German army to act as enemy forces to increase their realism.

Once 12 Armoured Brigade completed its involvement in Exercise Steadfast Defender 2024, it began preparing to become the lead armoured brigade in 2025 and be held at readiness to respond to unexpected events.

LEFT: The Royal Tank Regiment will remain as the brigade's sole armoured unit after the King's Royal Hussars convert to the Ajax reconnaissance vehicle later this decade. (MOD/CROWN COPYRIGHT)

BELOW: Soldiers from the Royal Welsh Regiment practiced river assaults during Exercise Immediate Response in Poland in May 2024. (MOD/CROWN COPYRIGHT)

20 Armoured Brigade

The Iron Fist

20 Armoured Brigade Combat Team (BCT) has a distinguished history, going back more than 70 years when it was formed at the height of the Cold War as part of the British Army of the Rhine. Until 2019, it had been based exclusively in Germany and was the last British Army formation to be based on continental Europe.

Today, it is one of two brigade-sized armoured formations in 3 (UK) Division and is currently overseeing the deployment of British troops in

Estonia to protect the Baltic state. From next year it will take the lead in bringing many new vehicles and weapons into service to accelerate the re-equipping of the British Army.

Its current headquarters is at Bulford, Wiltshire and the brigade's major units are based close by on Salisbury Plain.

The brigade's main striking power is provided by the Challenger 2 main battle tanks of the Queen's Royal Hussars. The regiment is nicknamed 'Churchill's Own' in honour of Britain's famous prime minister, Winston Churchill, who joined one its predecessor regiments, the 4th Hussars, and was later its regimental colonel from 1941 to 1965. It has been earmarked to be the first armoured regiment to receive the upgraded Challenger 3 main battle tank after it enters service in around three years' time.

Unlike its sister BCT, 20 Armoured Brigade already has its own armoured reconnaissance regiment, and this is already preparing to re-equip with the Ajax family of armoured vehicles. The Royal Dragoon Guards (RDG) are currently equipped with Warrior infantry fighting vehicles and Jackal patrol vehicles to prepare the regiment for the arrival of the Ajax. It is using the Warrior as a surrogate

Ajax to help develop the tactics and procedures that will be used with the new vehicle.

The main armoured infantry force of the brigade is provided by the Royal Regiment of Fusiliers and the Rifles. Both of the brigades armoured infantry battalions are currently equipped with the Warrior vehicle. These units will start handing over their long serving Warriors next year and they will then begin training on the new Boxer wheeled armoured personnel carrier. The 1st Battalion, Royal Regiment of Fusiliers (1 RRF), is scheduled to be the first unit to receive the Boxer, and personnel have already been carrying out early work on these vehicles to develop new tactics and procedures to be used with it.

A light role infantry battalion from the Princess of Wales's Royal Regiment (PWRR) is scheduled to move to Salisbury Plain to join the brigade in 2026.

In wartime, its regular army soldiers are to be reinforced by three army reserve infantry battalions from the Rifles, RRF, and the PWRR. These units are intended to reinforce the regular infantry battalions and provide rear area security for the brigade. The tank crews of the Queen's Royal Hussars are also earmarked to be reinforced by soldiers from the Royal Wessex Yeomanry in time of war.

To make the brigade self-contained on operations, it is augmented by a logistic support group. It is led by 1 Regiment RLC and also contains 1 Regiment RAMC and 3 Battalion REME.

As a result of its long presence in Germany, the brigade has »

20 Armoured Brigade Combat Team	
Headquarters & Signals Squadron	Bulford Camp
Armoured Regiment (Challenger 2)	
Queen's Royal Hussars	Assaye Barracks, Tidworth
Armoured Cavalry Regiment (Warrior/Jackal)	
Royal Dragoon Guards	Battlesbury Barracks, Warminster
Armoured Infantry Battalion (Warrior/Bulldog)	
5th Battalion, Rifles	Ward Barracks, Bulford
1st Battalion, Royal Regiment of Fusiliers	Mooltan Barracks, Tidworth
Light-role Infantry Battalion	
3rd Battalion, Rifles (to 11 SFA Brigade 2024)	Dreghorn Barracks, Edinburgh
Infantry Battalion (Army Reserve)	
3rd Battalion, Princess of Wales's Royal Regiment	Canterbury
5th Battalion, Royal Regiment of Fusiliers	Alnwick
7th Battalion, Rifles	Kensington
Logistic Support Group	
1 Medical Regiment RAMC	Bhutpore Barracks, Tidworth
1 Regiment RLC	St David's Barracks, Bicester
3 (Armoured Close Support) REME Battalion	Jellalabad Barracks, Tidworth

LEFT: A battery of MLRS launchers was placed under the command of the 20 Armoured Brigade's battlegroup in Estonia.
(MOD/CROWN COPYRIGHT)

BELOW: 20 Armoured Brigade is home based on Salisbury Plain and uses the training areas extensively to prepare for overseas deployments.
(MOD/CROWN COPYRIGHT)

RIGHT: 1st Battalion, The Royal Regiment of Fusiliers are one of 20 Armoured Brigade's two armoured infantry battalions. (NATO)

BELOW: The Queen's Own Royal Hussars are nicknamed 'Churchill's Own' because of their historic links to Britain's famous wartime leader, Winston Churchill. (MOD/CROWN COPYRIGHT)

a close association with NATO. After tension started to rise with Russia after the 2014 occupation of Crimea its operations became increasingly orientated to Eastern Europe. In 2017, it was the inaugural NATO Very High Readiness Joint Task Force (Land) (VJTF(L)), which had the mission of deploying anywhere in Europe in response to rising tension or war. In this role it placed the brigade headquarters in command of 5,000 British and allied troops, including Danish and British armoured infantry, Polish mechanised infantry, a US aviation battalion, Spanish light mechanised infantry, and a British-led multinational light-role infantry battalion.

20 Armoured Brigade's current main effort is to provide the battlegroup-sized British military contingent in Estonia and in time of crisis rapidly reinforce the Baltic state. The Forward Land Forces (FLF) commitment was enhanced in the spring of 2022 after the start of the Ukraine War when NATO nations promised to upscale their contingents in the three Baltic states from battlegroup to brigade size. Unlike Germany and Canada who moved additional troops to Lithuania and Latvia, Britain earmarked a

brigade to rapidly reinforce Estonia if war looms.

Under the LFF concept, 20 Armoured Brigade hold units at readiness to rapidly move to Sennelager in Germany to take over armoured vehicles held in storage. Other troops and vehicles can be moved directly to Estonia on Point-class, roll-on, roll-off ships. RAF aircraft can also move troops to Estonia by air if needed.

The soldiers of 20 Brigade have built up an unprecedented level of experience operating in Estonia, since they first deployed there in 2017 when the 5th Battalion, The Rifles (5 RIFLES) was the first British battlegroup to serve in the Baltic state.

Since early 2023 it has had the FLF commitment and has rotated battlegroups to Camp Tapa in Estonia for six-month tours of duty. Currently, 5 RIFLES are on duty in Estonia, but in the autumn a novel development will take place when the RDG takes the lead. This will be the first time that an armoured reconnaissance regiment has led the Estonia battlegroup, and it will allow tactical experimentation to take place.

Once the RDG finish their six-month tour of duty, 4 Light Brigade are scheduled to take over the FLF commitment to allow 20 Armoured Brigade to turn its attention to bringing its new vehicles and equipment into service.

20 Armoured Brigade History

20 Armoured Brigade can trace its history back to the pre-World War Two as 20th Light Armoured Brigade of the Territorial Army. The formation never saw action and was disbanded in 1943.

It was reformed in 1950 as Cold War tension with the Soviet Union was escalating and the brigade moved to Germany in December 1951. It remained in the British Army of the Rhine for nearly 70 years. After 1990, the British Army started to deploy forces on peacekeeping missions around the world and 20 Armoured Brigade pulled its fair share of these operational tours, starting in 1995 when it went to Bosnia for six months. Two more tours to Bosnia followed and then it served in Iraq three times between 2003 and 2009. It then served in Afghanistan in 2011. These tours did not see the formation operate as an armoured brigade but it controlled troops on peacekeeping and humanitarian operations.

The brigade's badge was adopted from the Royal Armoured Corps 'fist' insignia in 1958 but it was only in 2008 that the nickname 'Iron Fist' came into widespread use.

Warrior Infantry Fighting Vehicle	
In service:	1984 to present
Used by:	British Army and Kuwait
Manufacturer:	GKN Sankey, GKN Defence, Alvis
Produced:	1984 to 1995
Number built:	789 built, 623 still held by the British Army in 2024
Specifications (FV510 Warrior Infantry Section Vehicle)	
Mass:	25.4 tonnes
Length:	6.3m (20ft 8in)
Width:	3.03m (9ft 11in)
Height:	2.8m (9ft 2in)
Crew:	Three (commander, gunner, driver) + seven troops
Armour:	Aluminium and appliqué
Main armament:	30mm L21A1 RARDEN cannon
Secondary armament:	Coaxial 7.62mm L94A1 chain gun, 7.62mm machine gun
Engine:	Perkins V-8 Condor Diesel
Maximum speed:	46mph (75 kph) on road, 31mph (50 kph) off road

ABOVE: French and Danish troops serve alongside 20 Armoured Brigade units in the NATO Enhanced Forward Presence battlegroup in Estonia in 2023 and 2024. (MOD/CROWN COPYRIGHT)

LEFT: When the Ajax is fully in service, 20 Armoured Brigade will have an armoured cavalry regiment equipped with the reconnaissance vehicle. (MOD/CROWN COPYRIGHT)

1 Deep Recce Strike Brigade

Winning the Deep Battle

This unique formation was stood up in July 2022 and it's designed to provide the British Army with the ability to find and destroy targets deep behind enemy lines.

It brings together rocket, artillery, and reconnaissance systems under a single commander to allow firepower to be concentrated on key targets, wherever they are on the battlefield.

The formation is officially titled, 1 Deep Reconnaissance Strike Brigade Combat Team, and it controls more than a dozen major units.

Its heavy firepower is provided by two regiments equipped with the Multiple Launch Rocket Systems (MLRS) which currently fire the

guided, or GMLRS, rocket. Under its £2bn Land Deep Fires Programme, the Royal Artillery intends to increase its launcher numbers from 44 to 75 by the end of the decade. An expanded portfolio of rockets is also being procured to give commanders more strike options.

The British Army MLRS launchers will be upgraded to the M270A2 standard, which includes a number of British-specific upgrades such as new composite rubber tracks, radar, and video sensors, as well as a developed fire control. Britain is buying the Precision Strike Missile (PrSM) weapon, which is replacing US MLRS rockets. It carries a newly designed area-effects warhead and has a range of 60–499 kilometres. PrSM missiles can be launched from the M270A2, with rockets pods containing two of the weapons. The GMLRS-Extended Range rocket variant, which has a range of 150km, is also on order.

Alongside the procurement of GMLRS-Extended Range and the PrSM, Britain is also developing two additional rockets under its 'one launcher, many payloads' concept. These include the Dispensing-Rocket Payload and Land Precision Strike.

The Royal Artillery's two 155mm self-propelled gun regiments are also concentrated in the brigade

1 Deep Strike Recce Brigade Combat Team	
Headquarters & Signals Squadron	Delhi Barracks, Tidworth
Deep Strike Regiment (MLRS)	
3rd Regiment Royal Horse Artillery	Albemarle Barracks, Newcastle
26 Regiment RA	Purvis Lines, Larkhill Garrison
101 Regiment RA (Army Reserve)	Gateshead
Armoured Close Support Regiment (AS90/Archer)	
1st Regiment Royal Horse Artillery	Purvis Lines, Larkhill Garrison
19 Regiment RA	Purvis Lines, Larkhill Garrison
104 Regiment RA (Army Reserve)	Newport
Armoured Cavalry Regiment (Warrior/Jackal)	
Household Cavalry Regiment (Ajax from 2025)	Ward Barracks, Bulford
Royal Lancers	Cambrai Barracks, Catterick
Light Cavalry Regiment (Jackal)	
1st Queen's Dragoon Guards	Robertson Barracks, Dareham
Royal Yeomanry Regiment (Army Reserve)	Leicester
Surveillance Target Acquisition	
5 Regiment RA	Marne Barracks, Catterick (to Larkhill)
Repair Battalion	
6 (Close Support) Battalion REME	Delhi Barracks, Tidworth

but a major re-equipment project is underway with the current AS90s being retired early in 2025. The first stage of the retirement process started earlier in May when 1st Regiment Royal Horse Artillery (1RHA) fired its last live rounds in the UK on Salisbury Plain. After its last battery completes a nine-month operation tour in Estonia, the remaining six guns will be retired. The remaining fleet of less than 30 guns, as well as the remaining spare parts stockpile, will then be handed over to the Ukrainian army.

The Royal Artillery is currently bringing its interim buy of 14 Archer 155mm guns into service and it will have to make do with them for close fire support until the first Remote-Controlled Howitzer 155mm (RCH 155) 52 calibre Wheeled Artillery Systems come online later in the decade.

To find targets for its guns, the brigade has two armoured reconnaissance or cavalry regiments, a light cavalry regiment and the Royal Artillery's surveillance and acquisition regiment. The armoured cavalry regiments are in the process of being re-equipped with the new Ajax family of vehicles, but progress has been slow due technical problems.

The brigade's rocket and gun regiments are each augmented in time of war by reserve regiments, who provide additional batteries and individual personnel when mobilised.

ABOVE: The long serving AS90 155mm self-propelled guns are all to be retired by early 2025. (MOD/CROWN COPYRIGHT)

LEFT: The wheeled Archer system will require the Royal Artillery to develop new tactics and procedures. (MOD/CROWN COPYRIGHT)

7 Air Defence Group

Recent conflicts in Ukraine and the Middle East have highlighted the importance of ground-based air defence (GBAD). After the end of the Cold War in 1990 it became very much a 'Cinderella' capability, but a decade ago the Royal Artillery began programmes to re-capitalise its main air defence weapons and supporting systems.

Currently, two Royal Artillery regiments are assigned to provide GBAD and they are both assigned to 7 Air Defence Group. It was set up in April 2019 with all the UK's ground-based air defence assets under its command. The group has since passed to 3 (UK) Division and is now based at Baker Barracks in Hampshire, where all its component units are based.

Air defence of the Falkland Islands is currently provided by a single battery of the Sky Sabre medium air defence system, developed by the European company MBDA, which replaced the old Rapier missiles in 2021. The weapon is known as Land Ceptor and is based on the Common

7 Air Defence Group	
Headquarters	Baker Barracks, Thorney Island
Short Range Air Defence (High Velocity Missile)	
12 Regiment RA	Baker Barracks, Thorney Island
106 Regiment RA (Army Reserve)	Baker Barracks, Thorney Island
Medium Range Air Defence (Sky Sabre)	
16 Regiment RA	Baker Barracks, Thorney Island

Anti-air Modular Missile (CAMM), which has been successfully used in the Red Sea by the Royal Navy.

Sky Sabre is operated by 16 Regiment RA and its four batteries take turns to deploy to the South Atlantic. A project is underway to buy additional launchers and support systems to allow additional batteries to be equipped so the regiment will be able to provide an air defence umbrella for 3 (UK) Division on operations in Europe. The regiment also has the Giraffe-Agile Multi Beam (G-AMB) radar that provides early warning of aircraft and missile threats over the battlefield. 49 (Inkerman) Battery RA has the role Land Environment Air Picture Provision (LEAPP) and as well as operating the Giraffe radar shares the 'air picture' in real-time via computer networks with multiple headquarters, missile batteries and allied aircraft.

Point air defence is the responsibility of 12 Regiment RA, which is equipped with the Thales Starstreak High Velocity Missile (HVM). This is guided to its target by a laser beam. The Royal Artillery operates two versions. Its man portable or 'manpad' variant can be carried by dismounted soldiers and is usually assigned to support light forces, such as airborne units of 16 Air Assault Brigade. There is also a self-propelled version, known as Stormer, which has eight missiles in a rotating turret. Stormer equipped detachments are assigned to protect armoured battlegroups. In 2023, an additional battery was formed

LEFT: Armoured battlegroups are provided with self-propelled Stormer vehicles equipped with HVM. (MOD/CROWN COPYRIGHT)

because of an increased demand for air defence capability.

Both versions of HVM have been supplied to the Ukrainian military since 2022 and have reportedly shot down several Russian aircraft, helicopters, and drones.

Since 2020, 7 Air Defence Group has deployed detachments to the Middle East to help defend key allies against air and missile threats. In February 2020, two Giraffe radars were deployed to Saudi Arabia to help protect key infrastructure from Houthi attack drones launched from Yemen. They were replaced in early 2022 by a detachment of Stormer

Sky Sabre/Land Ceptor Surface-to-Air Missile	
In service	2021–present
Used by	British Army, Poland
Manufacturer	MBDA
Produced	2014 to date
Specifications (CAMM weapon)	
Mass	99kg (218lb)
Length	3.2m (10ft 6in)
Warhead	Directed fragmentation
Engine	Solid-fuel rocket motor
Operational range	CAMM: <1–25km (0.6–15.5 miles)+
Maximum speed	Mach 3; 1,020m/s (2,300mph)
Guidance system	Two-way data link, active radio frequency seeker

Starstreak High Velocity Missile (HVM)	
In service	1997–present
Used by	UK, Indonesia, Malaysia, South Africa, Thailand
Manufacturer	Thales Air Defence, formerly Shorts Missile Systems
Produced	1986 to date
Number built	In excess of 7,000
Length	1.397m (4ft 7in)
Warhead	Three explosive sub-munitions or darts
Warhead weight	3 × 0.90kg (2lb) tungsten alloy darts
Burnout maximum speed	More than Mach 4 at second stage

vehicles. A growing threat from Iranian-based militia groups in Iraq prompted the deployment of manpad HVM to British and coalition bases in the country in 2023. In December 2023, 170 (Imjin) Battery RA shot down an Iranian-made attack drone over Iraq in the first successful engagement of an enemy aircraft in combat since the 1982 Falklands war.

LEFT: The Sky Sabre is the British Army's newest air defence system. (MOD/CROWN COPYRIGHT)

Armoured Engineers

25 (Close Support) Engineer Group

RIGHT: Armoured engineering vehicles are used by the Royal Engineers in forward combat zones.
(MOD/CROWN COPYRIGHT)

BELOW: Trojan armoured engineering vehicles are operated exclusively by the units of 25 Engineer Group.
(MOD/CROWN COPYRIGHT)

Combat engineering is a highly specialised task, and the British Army has formed dedicated units to carry out this important mission. The British Army first formed specialist armoured engineering units in the run up to D-Day in 1944 to help it storm Hitler's heavily fortified Atlantic Wall. A whole family of armoured engineering, bridge-laying, amphibious and assault vehicles were developed by the commander of the 79th Armoured Division, Major General Percy Hobart. They became known as 'Hobart's Funnies'.

The modern successor of the 79th Armoured Division is the Bulford-based 25 (Close Support) Engineer Group, and it has two armoured engineer regiments, equipped with specialist engineering vehicles.

The Trojan armoured engineer vehicle is designed to open routes

25 (Close Support) Engineer Group	
Headquarters	Bulford Camp
Armoured Close Support	
22 Regiment RE	Swinton Barracks, Pernham Down
26 Regiment RE	Swinton Barracks, Pernham Down
Force Support	
21 Regiment RE	Claro Barracks, Ripon
Royal Monmouth RE (Army Reserve)	Monmouth

matter of minutes to form bridges or ferries. When the last British troops were withdrawn from Germany in 2019, 23 Amphibious Engineer Squadron remained behind to form a joint bridging regiment with the German army.

LEFT: The M3 bridging rigs are operated by a joint UK-German bridging unit based in Germany. (MOD/CROWN COPYRIGHT)

LEFT: In 2023, the units of 25 Engineer Group staged a series of major exercises around Britain. (MOD/CROWN COPYRIGHT)

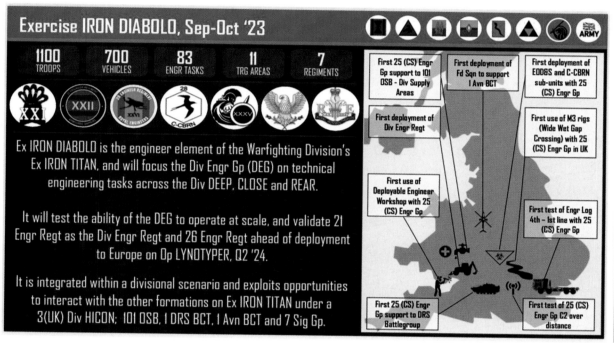

Exercise IRON DIABOLO, Sep-Oct '23

| 1100 TROOPS | 700 VEHICLES | 83 ENGR TASKS | 11 TRG AREAS | 7 REGIMENTS |

Ex IRON DIABOLO is the engineer element of the Warfighting Division's Ex IRON TITAN, and will focus the Div Engr Gp (DEG) on technical engineering tasks across the Div DEEP, CLOSE and REAR.

It will test the ability of the DEG to operate at scale, and validate 21 Engr Regt as the Div Engr Regt and 26 Engr Regt ahead of deployment to Europe on Op LYNOTYPER, Q2 '24.

It is integrated within a divisional scenario and exploits opportunities to interact with the other formations on Ex IRON TITAN under a 3(UK) Div HICON; 101 OSB, 1 DRS BCT, 1 Avn BCT and 7 Sig Gp.

First 25 (CS) Engr Gp support to 101 OSB - Div Supply Areas

First deployment of Fd Sqn to support 1 Avn BCT

First deployment of EOD&S and C-CBRN sub-units with 25 (CS) Engr Gp

First deployment of Div Engr Regt

First use of M3 rigs (Wide Wet Gap Crossing) with 25 (CS) Engr Gp in UK

First use of Deployable Engineer Workshop with 25 (CS) Engr Gp

First test of Engr Log 4th – 1st line with 25 (CS) Engr Gp

First 25 (CS) Engr Gp support to DRS Battlegroup

First test of 25 (CS) Engr Gp C2 over distance

BELOW: The BR90 bridging system is operated by 21 Regiment RE. (MOD/CROWN COPYRIGHT)

through complex battlefield obstacles and clear a path through minefields with specialist ploughs. It can also drop bundles of fascines to fill in anti-tank ditches. Trojan is based on the Challenger 2 main battle tank chassis.

The Terrier armoured digger is the Royal Engineer's dedicated engineering vehicle. It has a dozer bucket and a mechanical digger arm. It can also carry and deliver fascines. An operator can also operate the vehicle up to 1,000 metres away, if the vehicle needs to be used to clear paths through minefields and other dangerous terrain.

To cross gaps of up to 60 metres the Royal Engineers have the Titan bridge laying tank, which can carry and drop a selection of close support bridges. Like the Trojan, it is based on the Challenger 2 chassis.

Armoured engineer units are configured to be attached to armoured battlegroups so they can be closely integrated into their commander's plans. By having Trojan, Titan, and Terrier vehicles operating in the first echelon of armoured assaults it allows obstacles to be quickly crossed to maintain the momentum of the advance. Since 2017, an armoured engineering squadron has been maintained in Estonia as part of Britain's NATO Enhanced Forward Presence battlegroup.

Engineering support away from the frontline is provided by 21 Engineer Regiment RE, which is equipped to build field fortifications, camps, roads, and bridges to keep 3 (UK) Division moving forward. It also operates the M3 bridging rig, which is the Royal Engineers' 'wet gap crossing' capability. This unique system can either be operated as a ferry or several rigs can be combined to form a large bridge. The self-propelled rigs can be driven into rivers and then lashed together in a

101 Operational Sustainment Brigade

Vanguard Support Brigade

ABOVE: Keeping the British Army supplied with the ammunition, food, and supplies to keep fighting is the job of Royal Logistic Corps. (MOD/CROWN COPYRIGHT)

To keep 3 (UK) Division fighting it has its own dedicated logistic organisation, which is currently titled 101 Operational Sustainment Brigade. Up until 2024 it was known as 101 Logistic Brigade.

The brigade is configured to support 3 (UK) Division in high intensity combat operations, and its command group is designed to co-ordinate the storage and movement of supplies, evacuation of wounded soldiers, and the repair of damaged vehicles and equipment.

In the old days, military planners used to talk about of 'lines of communications' but many of these concepts have had to be updated to incorporate modern technology and new equipment.

RIGHT: Bulk fuel supplies are essential to keep tanks and other vehicles moving. (MOD/CROWN COPYRIGHT)

Modern armies consume vast quantities of fuel, ammunition, and other supplies and complex networks need to be established to keep these supplies flowing to the frontline.

After deploying to an operational theatre, 101 Brigade would first establish a series of 'administrative areas', or 'supply dumps' in old money, to collect ammunition, food, spare parts, fuel, and water. These are now stored on pallets or in ISO containers fitted with radio frequency (RF) tags, which in turn are all marked with bar codes so logistic planners can automatically track them as they are moved around the battlefield. Computerised tracking systems have been introduced so planners can monitor consumption of vital supplies and move items quickly to where they are needed.

These pallets and containers are moved forward to frontline units on MAN Support Vehicles and dropped off with battlegroup logistic echelons to distribute to combat units. Bulk fuel and water are moved forward in specialist Oshkosh tankers.

During mobile operations, supplies are loaded on to truck convoys to move just behind the forward battlegroups so they can be rapidly re-supplied to keep the advance moving at a rapid tempo. Rolling replenishment points will be set up so vehicles can drive through, collecting food and ammunition, from the back of supply trucks and they can be refuelled.

The Ukraine war has highlighted the vulnerability of supply columns to enemy air and missile strikes, so the British Army is evolving its logistic concepts to reduce their exposure to attack. At the heart of this is the idea of dispersing supply dumps and making re-supply convoys smaller so that if they are knocked out it does not lead to large quantities of valuable supplies being lost.

Tanks and other tracked vehicles are slow, and they have limited range, so the British Army has a fleet of Oshkosh Heavy Equipment Transporters (HETs) to move them over long distances. The British Army also has agreements with British and European railway companies so that heavy armoured vehicles can be moved rapidly by train on flat cars.

101 Brigade is also responsible for operating 3 (UK) Division's medical evacuation chain. Armoured ambulance or multi-role medical regiments can be attached, and their job is to collect wounded soldiers from regimental medical posts and evacuate them back to field hospitals, where they can be stabilised. These ambulance regiments have fleets of AFV432 configured to carry casualties, and they are soon to be replaced by ambulance variants of the Boxer armoured vehicle. Boeing Chinook heavy lift helicopters belonging to the Royal Air Force and carrying medical emergency response teams, or MERT, can also be used to move high priority casualties back to field hospitals. Once they are stabilised, casualties can be moved to airfields to be flown back to Britain to be treated by the National Health Service.

The brigade is held in high readiness and is described as a 'vanguard support brigade', with its major units ready to deploy at a few day's notice.

101 Operational Sustainment Brigade	
Headquarters	St Omar Barracks, Aldershot
Division Support Logistics	
10 Gurkha Regiment RLC	Gale Barracks, Aldershot
27 Regiment RLC	Travers Barracks, Aldershot
Transport Regiment (Army Reserve)	
151 Regiment RLC	Croydon
156 Regiment RLC	Liverpool
157 (Welsh) Regiment RLC	
Repair Battalions	
5 (Force Support) Battalion REME	Lyneham
103 (Force Support) Battalion REME (Army Reserve)	Northampton

1 (UK) Division

Global Role

1 (United Kingdom) Division is the British Army's 'global response' formation. It is a capable force that is able to respond across the spectrum of operations from humanitarian assistance and disaster relief to security operations and war fighting.

As a result of the 2021 Integrated Review, the British government decided that it was not enough to deploy troops to respond to crisis, but it was better to engage around the world to try to head off crisis escalating into open conflict.

This has led to the idea of 'persistent operations', with troops being constantly deployed overseas on exercises or training missions to help allied forces. It is the job of 1 (UK) Division to choreograph these operations from its headquarters in York. The division also has global hubs in Kenya, Brunei, Oman, and Belize, where large scale exercises take place and equipment is pre-positioned.

The division is the biggest formation in the British Army with nearly 30,000 troops under its command, drawn from eight brigades and dozens of other units.

'Downstream engagement' is the mission of the division's security force assistance brigade that is configured to dispatch training teams to help allied forces around the world. This brigade also played an important role in launching Operation Interflex in 2022 to train Ukrainian soldiers.

Since 2023, 1 (UK) Division has commanded the British Army's premier rapid reaction unit, 16 Air Assault Brigade Combat Team. Units of this brigade are on a few hours' notice to deploy to crisis overseas, leading to it being dubbed the 'global response force'. From July 2024, 1(UK) Division is to head the land component of NATO's Allied Response Force (ARF), at readiness to deploy in crisis situations.

The divisional headquarters moved to its current home at Imphal Barracks in York in 2015. Up until then, it had been the British Army's sole armoured division, based in Germany.

ABOVE: 7 Light Mechanised Brigade is assigned to NATO for the remainder of 2024 as the alliance's Very High Readiness Joint Task Force (Land) (VJTF(L)). (MOD/CROWN COPYRIGHT)

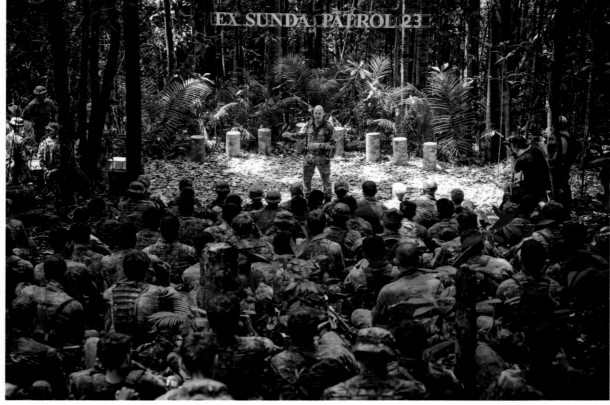

EX SUNDA PATROL 23

RIGHT: Units of 1 (UK) Division are trained to operate in a wide range of environments, from mountains to deserts and jungles. (MOD/CROWN COPYRIGHT)

Information Manoeuvre and More

The Specialists

I (UK) Division can draw on specialist support for its globally deployed units on operations or exercises.

Global communication support is provided by the York-based 2 Signals Regiment of the Royal Signals. It is configured to provide the division's command post or detachments to provide communications links to smaller troop contingents. Reservists from 37 Signals Regiment, headquartered in Redditch, are able to augment its regular counterparts.

Information on threats and geo-political trends is available from Intelligence Corps experts in the regular 1 Military Intelligence Battalion at Catterick and reservists of the Edinburgh-based 5 Military Intelligence Battalion.

The division has responsibility for the British Army's deployable military police formation, which has a key role providing security and traffic control for deployed contingents. The Andover-based 1 Military Police Brigade has two deployable units,

1 (UK) Division	
Headquarters	Imphal Barracks, York
Communications Units	
2 Signals Regiment	Imphal Barracks, York
37 Signals Regiment (Army Reserve)	Redditch
Information Manoeuvre Units	
1 Military Intelligence Battalion, IC	Bourlon Barracks, Catterick
5 Military Intelligence Battalion, IC (Army Reserve)	Edinburgh
1 Military Police Brigade	Marlborough Lines, Andover
1 Regiment RMP	Catterick
3 Regiment RMP	Bulford
Special Investigation Branch	Bulford
Special Operations Unit	Southwick Park
Military Provost Staff Corps	Colchester

1 and 3 Regiments RMP, as well as the Special Operations Regiment which investigates crimes by military personnel. The Military Provost Staff runs Britain's military prison at Colchester. The Royal Military Police branch comprises almost 2,500 regular and reserve personnel.

ABOVE: Satellite communications are an essential to allow 1 (UK) Division to operate around the world. (MOD/CROWN COPYRIGHT)

BELOW: Wildcat helicopters of the Army Air Corps are often detached to support 1 (UK) Division exercises in Oman. (MOD/CROWN COPYRIGHT)

7 Light Mechanised Brigade

The Desert Rats

RIGHT: Troops from 7 Mechanised Light Brigade were put through their paces as the Very High Readiness Joint Task Force (VJTF(L)) in Exercise Dragon 24 in February and March 2024.
(MOD/CROWN COPYRIGHT)

The brigade can trace its heritage back to the North Africa campaign of World War Two when 7th Armoured Division duelled with Rommel's Afrika Korps. It was nicknamed the Desert Rats, after its badge which features a red jerboa, a nocturnal rodent indigenous to North Africa. After World War Two, the brigade was reformed in

RIGHT: The heritage of the 'Desert Rats' lives on in the badge of 7 Mechanised Light Brigade.
(MOD/CROWN COPYRIGHT)

BELOW: Royal Anglian Regiment soldiers staged an assault river crossing during Exercise Dragon 24.
(MOD/CROWN COPYRIGHT)

Germany and adopted the division's famous red jerboa badge that is still used today.

In 2014, the brigade lost its armoured role as part of the drawdown of the British Army in Germany and then moved to its current home at Kendrew Barracks on the former site of RAF Cottesmore in Rutland. The 2021 Future Soldier plan saw the brigade re-roled from an infantry formation into its current incarnation, 7 Light Mechanised Brigade Combat Team (BCT).

In its new role, the new 7 Brigade is focused on operating on wheeled vehicles in the NATO area or further afield. It currently has a mix of infantry units, including light role or marching battalions, light mechanised battalions equipped with the small Foxhound mine protected vehicles, and a heavy mine protected battalion

7 Light Mechanised Brigade Combat Team	
Headquarters & Signals Squadron	Kendrew Barracks, Cottesmore
Light Mechanised Infantry Battalion (Foxhound)	
1st Battalion, Princess of Wales's Royal Regiment	RA Barracks, Woolwich (to close 2028)
2nd Battalion, Royal Anglian Regiment	Kendrew Barracks, Cottesmore
1st Battalion, Royal Yorkshire Regiment	Munster Barracks, Catterick
4th Battalion, Royal Regiment of Scotland	Bourlon Barracks, Catterick
Heavy Protected Infantry Battalion (Mastiff)	
1st Battalion, Scots Guards	Somme Barracks, Catterick
Light Armoured Cavalry Regiment (Jackal)	
Royal Scots Dragoon Guards	Waterloo Lines, Leuchars Station
Close Support Artillery Regiment (105mm Light Gun)	
4 Regiment RA	Alanbrooke Barracks, Topclife
105 Regiment RA (Army Reserve)	Edinburgh
32 Engineer Regimnent RE	Catterick
Logistic Support Group	
6 Regiment RLC	Dishforth Airfield
3 Medical Regiment RAMC	Gaza Barracks, Catterick
1 (Close Support) Battalion REME	Catterick Garrison

equipped with large Mastiff mine protected vehicles.

The brigade has its own light cavalry regiment that conducts reconnaissance missions in the Jackal 2 patrol vehicle. Fire support is provided by the 105mm Light Guns of 4 Regiment RA and its partner Army Reserve unit, 105 Regiment RA. Combat engineers from 32 Engineer Regiment RE are attached to the brigade to build field defences, build bridges, and construct camps.

Logistic support is provided by a Royal Logistic Corps regiment, the Royal Mechanical & Electrical Engineers, and a Royal Army Medical Corps ambulance regiment.

The brigade has the task of supplying the two infantry battalions for the Cyprus garrison and they rotate units back and forth for two-year-long tours of duty.

Between 2020 end the end of 2022, the brigade was responsible for providing the British contingent to the United Nations in the West African country of Mali. They patrolled around the African desert to deter attacks by insurgents.

In January 2024, 7 Brigade assumed a new role for a year as the lead headquarters in NATO's Very High Readiness Joint Task Force (Land) (VJTF(L)). This multi-national organisation is held at 72 hours' notice to deploy anywhere in the NATO area. The brigade took part in Exercise Steadfast Defender in February and March 2024 to test the VJHQ (L).

One of the brigade's infantry battalions is also held at high readiness to deploy overseas on national or NATO missions. In October 2023, the 1st Battalion, Princess of Wales' Regiment was rapidly deployed by air and sea to Kosovo as tension developed in the Balkan country.

ABOVE LEFT: Soldiers from the 2nd Battalion, Royal Anglian Regiment are one of 7 Brigade's five infantry battalions. (MOD/CROWN COPYRIGHT)

LEFT: Brigadier Guy Foden is the current commander of the Desert Rats. (MOD/CROWN COPYRIGHT)

BELOW: Foxhound mine protected vehicles are widely used to give the Desert Rats battlefield mobility. (MOD/CROWN COPYRIGHT)

4 Light Brigade

The Black Rats

RIGHT: The Black Rats insignia of 4 Brigade traces its heritage back to the North African campaign of World War Two. (MOD/CROWN COPYRIGHT)

The Catterick-based 4 Light Brigade Combat Team (BCT) is the British Army's premier infantry formation. It traces its roots back to the days of the 7th Armoured Division in North Africa during World War Two, when the brigade adopted the black jerboa insignia and hence became known as the 'Black Rats'.

During the Cold War it was an armoured brigade in the British Army of the Rhine (BAOR). It undertook peacekeeping duty with NATO in Bosnia in 1995-1996 and three years later it accompanied NATO troops into Kosovo. Tours of duty in Iraq and Afghanistan followed until it relocated from Germany to Catterick in 2014. Its conversion to an infantry brigade followed and it took its latest configuration in 2022. The brigade headquarters also has a secondary role as the British Army's regional

RIGHT: 4 Brigade infantry units regularly deploy to Brunei for jungle warfare training. (MOD/CROWN COPYRIGHT)

BELOW: The Light Dragoons are 4 Brigade's light cavalry regiment. In 2021 the regiment deployed on United Nations peacekeeping duty in Mali. (MOD/CROWN COPYRIGHT)

headquarters for the northeast of England.

From its Catterick headquarters, the brigade controls four regular light role or marching infantry battalions. They are trained in conventional infantry combat skills, and routinely deploy around the world to develop expertise in jungle, mountain, desert, forest, and urban combat environments. The brigade has the lead to run annual desert training in Oman under the banner of Exercise Khanjar Oman. These usually involve an infantry battalion and supporting elements, with around 1,000 troops in total taking part for several weeks at a time.

4 Brigade's units have undertaken operational deployments to Eastern Europe, Africa, and the Middle East. The 2nd Battalion, Royal Regiment of Scotland, is currently serving in Iraq in the force protection role.

The Light Dragons serve in the light cavalry role in the Jackal 2 patrol vehicle, providing the brigade with mobile firepower and reconnaissance capabilities. The regiment has undertaken operational tours in Mali with the United Nations, forming the core of a long-range desert patrol force. It has also served in Poland with NATO, deploying a squadron sized unit as part of a US-led battlegroup.

The brigade does not have assigned regular specialist support units so has to rely on the Army Reserve to provide a 105mm Light Gun regiment, an engineer regiment, a transport

4 Light Brigade Combat Team	
Headquarters & Signals Squadron	Peronne Lines, Catterick
Light--role Infantry Battalion	
2nd Battalion, Royal Regiment of Scotland	Edinburgh, Glencorse Barracks
1st Battalion, Grenadier Guards	Lille Barracks, Aldershot
1st Battalion, Coldstream Guards	Victoria Barracks Windsor
2nd Battalion, Rifles	Thiepval Barracks, Lisburn
Light Armoured Cavalry Regiment (Jackal)	
Light Dragoons	Gaza Barracks, Catterick
Close Support Artillery Regiment (105mm Light Gun)	
103 Regiment RA (Army Reserve)	St Helens
Close Support Engineer Regiment	
75 Engineer Regiment RE (Army Reserve)	Warrington
Logistic Support Group	
154 (Scottish) Regiment RLC (Army Reserve)	Dunfermline
102 Battalion (Close Support) Battalion REME (Army Reserve)	Newton Aycliffe

regiment, and an equipment repair battalion.

In 2025, the brigade is to take on the NATO Forward Land Forces (FLF) commitment and be at the heart of contingency planning to reinforce the NATO battle group in Estonia for two years. During the period, the brigade headquarters will stand ready to rapidly deploy to Estonia and take under command an array of British units operating in the Baltic state. These are expected to include tanks, artillery, and other specialist units. At some point during its FLF tenure, the brigade is expected to hold a major reinforcement exercise to test its plans for the defence of Estonia.

LEFT: 4 Brigade's infantry units are equipped with a range of non-standard small arms including variants of the US-made AR-15. (MOD/CROWN COPYRIGHT)

BELOW: Desert warfare training in Oman and Jordan is regularly on the agenda for 4 Brigade's units. (MOD/CROWN COPYRIGHT)

16 Air Assault Brigade

Global Response Force

Britain's airborne forces are now grouped together in 16 Air Assault Brigade Combat Team (BCT), headquartered at Melville Barracks in Colchester.

The brigade has built a reputation as one of Britain's toughest combat formations thanks to a series of successful operations over the past 25 years. It is currently described as the British Army's 'global response force' and it is held at high readiness to respond to crises around the world. The brigade's troops are trained and equipped to deploy by air-landing, parachute, and helicopter.

16 Brigade's core role is to maintain and command the Air Manoeuvre Task Force (AMTF), comprising infantry, aviation, and support units held at very high readiness to deploy anywhere in the world to carry out the full spectrum

16 Air Assault Brigade Combat Team	
Headquarters & 216 Signals Squadron	Merville Barracks, Colchester
Pathfinders	Merville Barracks, Colchester
Airborne Infantry Battalion	
2nd Battalion, Parachute Regiment	Merville Barracks, Colchester
3rd Battalion, Parachute Regiment	Hyderabad Barracks, Colchester
4th Battalion, Parachute Regiment (Army Reserve)	Pudsey, Leeds
Air Assault Infantry Battalion	
1st Battalion, Royal Gurkha Rifles	Sir John Moore Barracks, Folkstone
Light Strike Recce Battalion	
1st Battalion, Royal Irish Regiment	Clive Barracks, Ternhill (to close 2025-27)
Close Support Artillery Regiment	
7th Parachute Regiment Royal Horse Artillery	Merville Barracks, Colchester
Airborne Logistic Regiment	
13 Air Assault Regiment RLC	Merville Barracks, Colchester
Airborne Medical Regiment	
16 Medical Regiment RAMC	Merville Barracks, Colchester
Airborne Engineer Regiment	
23 Parachute Engineer Regiment RE	Rock Barracks, Woodbridge

of missions, from non-combatant evacuation operations (NEO) to war fighting. The AMTF is a scalable organisation that can draw on units and personnel of 16 Brigade, which are held at readiness to deploy at short notice.

A full battalion of paratroops has to provide the first wave of 16 Brigade's troops in less than 24 hours of getting the 'go command'. It is dubbed the Air Manoeuvre Battlegroup (AMBG). If enough warning is available, its readiness can be raised to 12 hours' notice to be ready to be 'wheels up' from RAF Brize Norton on getting the 'go command'. The full brigade aims to be on the ground in operational theatres within seven days.

The unique combat capability of 16 Brigade is dubbed 'theatre entry' by the British Army and this concept involves the ability to seize an airfield in an operational theatre, to allow following reinforcements to flow in. This can be either as part of a combat mission to take the fight to the enemy behind their lines or as part of a

NEO or a humanitarian operation in unstable countries.

After the first wave of assault troops secure an airhead, 16 Brigade contains all the necessary personnel and equipment to run the airfield to allow fixed wing transport aircraft and helicopters to begin to operate. Its logistics experts can then organise the delivery of supplies, humanitarian aid, or evacuation of refugees.

In war fighting operations, 16 Brigade is the British Army's lead formation for air manoeuvre operations to bring together fixed wing strike aircraft, attack helicopters, artillery, helicopter-borne troops, ground combat units and fixed wing transport aircraft into a single force. British air manoeuvre operations involve rapid movement to keep the enemy off balance and strike at key targets behind enemy »

LEFT: RAF A400M Atlas airlifters were finally cleared this year to carry out static line parachuting, restoring the airborne capability to 16 Brigade after a gap of nearly a year caused by the retirement on cost grounds of the C-130J Hercules in 2023. (MOD/CROWN COPYRIGHT)

BELOW: Static line parachuting out of the side doors of a A400M Atlas allows hundreds of paratroopers to be delivered rapidly onto drop zones. (MOD/CROWN COPYRIGHT)

105mm Light Gun	
In service	1976 to present
Used by	British Army and 19 other armies globally
Manufacturer	Royal Ordnance
Produced	1976-1987
Number built	126 in use by the British Army in 2024
Specifications	
Mass	1,858kg (4,096lb)
Length	8.8m (28ft 10in)
Width	1.78m (5ft 10in)
Height	2.13m (7ft)
Crew	Six (normal), four (reduced)
Rate of fire	6–8 rounds per minute
Maximum firing range	17,200m (18,800 yards) 20,600m (22,500 yards) extended range using base bleed

RIGHT: 16 Air Assault Brigade routinely practices parachute drops in different environments, such as the deserts of Jordan, to maintain its operational skills.
(MOD/CROWN COPYRIGHT)

lines. At the heart of its operations is the rapid regrouping of units and personnel into ad hoc battlegroups for specific missions, to capitalise on their unique capabilities.

16 Brigade's headquarters and 216 Signals Squadron are held at high readiness to lead any short notice operations and a sizeable section of their personnel are parachute trained to jump into operational theatres. Not all members of 16 Brigade are members of the Parachute Regiment but brigade personnel with an airborne role have to pass the all-arms parachute course and win their

Airborne History

Britain's airborne forces trace their history back to 1940 when Prime Minister Winston Churchill ordered the formation of an elite parachute unit to take the war to Nazi occupied Europe. Since then, its battle honours have become legendary – Normandy, Arnhem, Suez, and the Falklands are few of them. In 1999, the British Army airborne and airmobile brigades were combined to form 16 Air Assault Brigade. It then saw action in Iraq and Afghanistan. More recently it spearheaded the evacuation operation from Kabul in August 2021.

BELOW: RAF A400M Atlas carry out tactical air landing training on Pembrey Sands in South Wales with 16 Brigade's Pathfinder Platoon.
(MOD/CROWN COPYRIGHT)

parachute wings and the right to wear the covered maroon beret.

The brigade has four regular infantry battalions. Two are airborne units drawn from the Parachute Regiment, one is an air assault unit that is trained and equipped to move by aircraft or helicopter and the fourth unit is dubbed a light strike battalion. An Army Reserve Parachute Regiment battalion is

available to reinforce the brigade in time of war.

All Parachute Regiment personnel have to be jump qualified and are trained to carry out low level static parachuting from Royal Air Force Airbus A400M Atlas airlifters. Each of the regular parachute battalions takes turns to be the high readiness AMBG.

The 1st Battalion, Royal Gurkha Rifles, are currently 16 Brigade's air assault unit and stand ready to carry tactical air landing operations from fixed wing aircraft or helicopter assault missions.

Ground operations in vehicles are the speciality of the 1st Battalion, Royal Irish Regiment, which has the light strike role. It is trained and equipped to launch rapid raids against enemy positions and call in air and artillery fire.

Ground based firepower is provided by the 105mm Light Guns of 7th Regiment Royal Horse Artillery, whose guns can be underslung beneath RAF Boeing Chinook heavy lift helicopters. The guns will eventually be able to be air dropped by parachute from the RAF's Airbus A400M Atlas.

To enable its operations in all domains, 16 Brigade has its own combat engineer, logistic, and medical regiments. Each of these regiments has to provide a parachute trained contingent at high readiness to support the AMTF.

Air manoeuvre operations are only possible with the support of Royal Air Force and Army Air Corps aircraft and helicopters. 16 Brigade is usually assigned an aviation task force headquarters to control its attack and transport helicopters. Fixed wing transport aircraft are controlled by a RAF command team attached to 16 Brigade headquarters. RAF Regiment teams act as air controllers on airfields, guiding aircraft into land and marshalling them on the ground. Detachments from the RAF Air Mobility Wing unload transport aircraft and organise passengers to board them.

To maintain its air manoeuvre skills, 16 Brigade conducts annual exercises around the UK and Europe practicing a range of operations from NEOs to full warfighting missions. These are conducted in co-ordination with Britain's Permanent Joint Headquarters (PJHQ), which controls all UK overseas military operations, and its crisis response teams from the Joint Force Headquarters, which deploy to foreign crisis zones.

Operation Pitting, the evacuation of British passport holders and refugees from Afghanistan in 2021, saw 16 Brigade tested to the full. It deployed by air to Kabul and joined the US-led operation to secure the city's airport and then helped load more than 16,000 civilians onto RAF aircraft to be evacuated.

During 2023, 16 Brigade was in action again. Its 16 Medical Regiment RAMC led a humanitarian task force to Turkey in February to help rescue survivors from an earthquake that devastated much of the south of the country. The full AMTF was mobilised in April 2023 when a NEO

was ordered to rescue British passport holders from war-torn Sudan. It flew to RAF Akrotiri on Cyprus and stood ready to parachute into Sudan if the airfield being used for the evacuation was put out of action. In the end they did not need to jump, but a contingent of paratroopers flew into Port Sudan airport to operate an evacuation hub.

ABOVE: In May 2024, 16 Brigade took part in a live firing exercise in Estonia. (MOD/CROWN COPYRIGHT)

LEFT: 16 Brigade remains at high readiness, 24/7/365 to react to unexpected crises around the world. (MOD/CROWN COPYRIGHT)

11 Security Force Assistance Brigade

Winning Influence

During the wars in Iraq and Afghanistan, the British Army learned the critical lesson that training and advising local armies and militia forces has to be given a high priority. Locally recruited forces know the ground and their enemies, so providing them with military skills and expertise can have a disproportionate impact.

The British Army decided that it needed a dedicated organisation to provide training to local forces. It was recognised that training and advisory troops required very specific skill sets, such as languages and fire range safety qualifications, which are not usually available in line infantry battalions.

The 2021 Future Soldier plan gave this mission to the Aldershot-based 11 Infantry Brigade and re-roled it as 11 Security Force Assistance (SFA) Brigade. Its mission "is to draw on personnel and expertise from across the British Army, to build the capacity of allied and partner nations. By routinely deploying around the world, Security Force Assistance units contribute to conflict prevention and resilience at an early stage."

It is envisaged that the brigade will eventually have four regular SFA battalions, which are former light role infantry units that are being re-roled. These have a strength of

around 250 personnel compared to the 550 soldiers who are assigned to a traditional infantry battalion. These SFA units are officer and senior non-commissioned officer heavy, in recognition of their need to have personnel qualified to run live firing ranges or advise senior local commanders on tactics.

To assist the brigade's training teams, it has an outreach and cultural support organisation who provide them with intelligence and other information on the situation on the ground in operational theatres. A reserve infantry unit, the 4th Battalion, Prince of Wales's Royal

11 Security Force Assistance Brigade	
Headquarters	Taurus House, Aldershot
Security Assistance Force Battalions	
1st Battalion, Irish Guards	Mons Barracks, Aldershot
3rd Battalion, Royal Regiment of Scotland	Fort George, Inverness (to close 2025)
1st Battalion, Royal Anglian Regiment	Kendrew Barracks, Cottesmore
4th Battalion, Princess of Wales's Royal Regiment (Army Reserve)	Redhill
Support Units	
Outreach and Cultural Support	Hermitage, Reading

11 SFA Brigade was given the mission to launch Operation Interflex and set up a training operation across army bases in Britain and begin receiving Ukrainians in a matter of weeks. The brigade first used its own SFA battalions, but the task was so huge that other British Army units, assisted by personnel from across NATO and the Commonwealth, were mobilised.

Operation Interflex was a huge undertaking. Ukrainian soldiers had to be collected from Poland and flown to Britain by the RAF. The 11 SFA Brigade had to organise their transport to training bases, where training teams would put them through a crash programme in combat skills for six weeks. At its peak, around 900 Ukrainians a month were arriving in Britain to begin training. In 2023, the British government committed to training more than 20,000 more Ukrainian soldiers. As a result, 11 SFA Brigade handed the mission over to other parts of the British Army to run Operation Interflex on a near permanent basis.

ABOVE: Since June 2022, Ukrainian troops have been flown to Britain by the RAF to undergo intensive training. (MOD/CROWN COPYRIGHT)

LEFT: Lifesaving medical skills are a high priority during the training of Ukrainian soldiers in Britain. (MOD/CROWN COPYRIGHT)

BELOW: Strong bonds now exist been Ukrainian troops and their British instructors. (MOD/CROWN COPYRIGHT)

Regiment, can augment the brigade in time of conflict or a major crisis.

Soon after the brigade was established it was given responsibility for the mission to train the Ukrainian army, codenamed Operation Orbital, dispatching training teams to the Eastern European country. After Russian forces invaded Ukraine in February 2022, the British government decided to ramp up support for Kyiv's military. The biggest priority was to train the Ukrainian army so it could fight off the invasion. This led to the launch in June 2022 of Operation Interflex to initially bring 10,000 Ukrainian troops to Britain to be trained.

19 Brigade

The Army's Reserve

RIGHT: The Duke of Lancaster's Regiment were represented at 19 Brigade's formation parade in July 2022.
(MOD/CROWN COPYRIGHT)

BELOW: Infantry skills are at the heart of 19 Brigade's training programme.
(MOD/CROWN COPYRIGHT)

The British Army has a long tradition of calling on reserves to augment its regular units in time of war.

Former regular, or professional soldiers, have a 'reserve commitment' to be recalled to duty in time of crisis but they rarely take part in training and are not allocated to serve in a specific unit on mobilisation. 'Army Reservists' are civilians or former soldiers who volunteer to train at weekends and are assigned to serve in formed units. These are the modern-day successors of the old Territorial Army (TA) volunteers. These so-called 'weekend warriors' were known as TA the until 2014, when they were re-branded as the Army Reserve.

Under plans to reform the Army Reserves in 2014, many units were designated as partners to regular units and on mobilisation their personnel would be assigned to serve in a specific regular unit.

For example, the Royal Wessex Yeomanry is designated to provide reinforcement tank crews to fill out the regular armoured regiments.

The reserve cavalry and infantry units that were not designated as partner organisations were assigned to a newly formed brigade that would be responsible for their training and operation.

The York-based 19 Brigade had the mission to prepare formed combat units to take their place in the British Army order of battle in time of crisis or war. The brigade has two light cavalry units, equipped with Jackal patrol vehicles to operate in the reconnaissance role. At its core are eight Army Reserve infantry battalions, and they are based around the United Kingdom.

The units are trained for conventional combat operations and their soldiers routinely spend one weekend each month training, as

19 Brigade	
Headquarters	York
Light Cavalry (Army Reserve)	
The Queen's Own Yeomanry	Newcastle
Scottish and North Irish Yeomanry	Edinburgh
Light-role Infantry Battalion (Army Reserve)	
3rd Battalion, Royal Anglian Regiment	Bury St Edmunds
6th Battalion, Royal Regiment of Scotland	Glasgow
7th Battalion, Royal Regiment of Scotland	Perth
4th Battalion, Duke of Lancaster's Regiment	Preston
4th Battalion, Royal Yorkshire Regiment	York
6th Battalion, Rifles	Exeter
8th Battalion, Rifles	Bishop Auckland
2nd Battalion, Royal Irish Regiment	Lisburn

well as undertaking a two week-long training camp each year.

Since 2023, Army Reserve infantry battalions have started to take up the slack from 11 SFA Brigade to train Ukrainian soldiers under Operation Interflex. For six-month periods at a time, these battalions have stood up to run the organisation, receiving and training Ukrainian troops in Britain.

19 Brigade's regiments are spread across the United Kingdom and their network of training centres provides the only military presence in many parts of the country. So, when natural disasters or emergencies occur, the reserves are often the first personnel who can be mobilised to help out providing 'Military Assistance to the Civil Authorities' (MACA) tasks. During the COVID-19 pandemic, reserve personnel were heavily involved in helping the test and trace effort, as well as assisting the National Health Service.

The Ministry of Defence is in the process of developing a National Defence and Resilience Plan to help protect the home base in the United Kingdom in time of war. The units of 19 Brigade are expected to be given an important role in this plan once it is finally approved by the government.

TOP LEFT: 19 Brigade can trace its history back to 1914 when it was formed in France. (MOD/CROWN COPYRIGHT)

ABOVE: Two Yeomanry light cavalry regiments equipped with the Jackal patrol vehicle are assigned to 19 Brigade. (MOD/CROWN COPYRIGHT)

LEFT: Infantry units of 19 Brigade are based around Britain and routinely exercise on their local training areas. (MOD/CROWN COPYRIGHT)

8 Engineer Brigade

Specialist Sappers

The Royal Engineers have a long tradition of building roads, bridges, and airfields around the world to help the British armed forces fight and win wars. Recent reorganisations have seen combat engineer units placed under the direct command of frontline brigades.

Specialist engineering capabilities have now been grouped together under 8 Engineer Brigade, headquartered at Minley in Hampshire. In turn it has three distinct groups. 12 Force Support Group, headquartered at RAF Wittering, has the mission to 'support to theatre entry, route maintenance, and enabling airfield operations'. This brings together many specialist skills and capabilities. Its two regular and one Army Reserve engineer regiments are trained and equipped to carry out basic construction of bridges, buildings, runways, helicopter landing pads, roads, aircraft hangers, and other infrastructure. They are assisted by 170 (Infrastructure Support) Engineer Group, which has four works groups, comprised of a number of Specialist Teams Royal Engineers (STRE), made up of experts, including surveyors, draftsmen and project managers. One of these works groups

is dedicated to building and repairing airfield infrastructure on behalf of the Royal Air Force. Three of the works groups are regular units and one is drawn from the Army Reserves. These groups also have the ability to contract civilian building companies or organisations to help in projects requiring specialist skills not readily available within the military.

To enable its operations, 8 Engineer Brigade has a network of plant and equipment depots where bridging and

other construction equipment is stored at high readiness for operations.

Bomb disposal has long been a key role of the Royal Engineers, stretching back to World War Two when Sappers defused German bombs dropped on British cities during the Blitz. Today, the role is termed Explosive Ordnance Disposal and Search (EOD&S) and is split between the Royal Engineers and Royal Logistic Corps (RLC). Experts from both corps are combined

8 Engineer Brigade	
Headquarters	Gibraltar Barracks, Minley
12 Force Support Group	RAF Wittering
36 (Queen's Gurkha Engineers) Regiment RE	Invicta Park Barracks, Maidstone
39 Regiment RE	Kinloss Barracks, Forres
71 Engineer Regiment RE (Army Reserve)	Leuchars Station
170 (Infrastructure Support) Engineer Group	
20 (Air Support) Works Group RE	RAF Wittering
62 Works Group RE	Chilwell, Nottingham
63 Works Group RE	Chilwell, Nottingham
65 Works Group RE (Army Reserve)	Chilwell, Nottingham
66 Works Group RE	Chilwell, Nottingham
29 EOD & Search Group	Carver Barracks, Wimbish
33 (EOD & Search) Regiment RE	Carver Barracks, Wimbish
35 (EOD & Search) Regiment RE	Carver Barracks, Wimbish
28 (Counter CBRN) Regiment RE	RAF Honington
Falcon Sqn RTR	Harman Lines, Warminster
101 (EOD & Search) Regiment RE (Army Reserve)	Catford
11 EOD Regiment RLC	Vauxhall Barracks, Didcot
1 Military Working Dog Regiment	St George's Barracks, North Luffenham

and threats. This role is shared with the RAF Regiment at its base at RAF Honington, where 28 Engineer Regiment RE is headquartered. Falcon Squadron of the Royal Tank Regiment is attached to carry out mobile CBRN reconnaissance in their Fuchs vehicles.

Search dogs make an important contribution to EOD&S operations and 1 Military Working Dog Regiment of the Royal Army Veterinary Corps provides these to Royal Engineers and RLC.

ABOVE: Engineering plant is used by sapper field squadrons to clear routes, build field fortifications, and prepare the foundations of buildings. (MOD/CROWN COPYRIGHT)

LEFT: Explosive ordnance disposal robots, popularly known as 'wheelbarrows', are used to make safe terrorist bombs and legacy ordnance from World War Two. (MOD/CROWN COPYRIGHT)

in 29 EOD&S Group, which headquartered at Didcot.

The RLC's 11 EOD Regiment is responsible for dealing with terrorist bombs and left over World War Two ordnance in the United Kingdom and it has detachments spread around Britain on alert to respond to bomb threats. Their white painted vans are familiar to the public and they are equipped with a series of robots to remotely deal with terrorist devices. The RLC first used these robots in Northern Ireland in the 1970s and they were soon nicknamed 'wheelbarrows'.

The group has two regular and one Army Reserve Royal Engineer EOD&S regiments, which are optimised for operating overseas to find insurgent improvised explosive devices that could threaten British troops.

The Royal Engineers are Britain's lead agency for dealing with chemical, biological, radioactive, and nuclear (CBRN) contamination

ABOVE: CBRN experts from 28 Engineer Regiment RE provide national capabilities to respond to chemical biological and radiological incidents. (MOD/CROWN COPYRIGHT)

102 Operational Sustainment Brigade

Global Logistics Power

RIGHT: ISO containers are used by the Royal Logistic Corps to rapidly move key equipment and supplies to the frontline. (MOD/CROWN COPYRIGHT)

BELOW: Supply convoys bring ammunition, food, and replacement equipment to frontline units. (MOD/CROWN COPYRIGHT)

The logistic support organisation of 1 (UK) Division is configured to operate far from the British home base on operations around the world. Unlike its counterpart that supports 3 (UK) Division during high intensity warfare in Europe, 102 Operational Sustainment Brigade is focused on supporting small contingents of troops in a wide range of environments, from jungles to deserts and mountains.

It is intended to be a light, agile force designed to receive both troops and equipment into the theatre of operations, organise their forward movement to the battle area along a line of communication that could be up to 750km long. They then have to logistically sustain fighting formations in a range of operations, before finally redeploying the force back to the UK base or on to subsequent operations.

This role involves complex logistic processes to deliver ammunition, fuel, and water to frontline units, as well as dealing with prisoners of war,

humanitarian assistance, rear area security, and medical operations.

The brigade has to be ready to respond to unexpected events and move rapidly to operational theatres, often working in co-operation with the UK's strategic theatre entry organisation, 104 Theatre Sustainment Brigade. Logistic units and key supplies are moved to operational theatres by RAF transport aircraft or the Ministry of Defence's roll-on, roll-off Point-class ships. 102 Brigade puts these procedures and techniques to the test on a regular basis during major exercises supporting 4 Light and 7 Light Mechanised Brigades.

4 Light Brigade runs a number of exercises each year in Oman under the Khanjar-series of training events. These usually involve a battalion-sized force of infantry deploying to the Duqm training base in Oman and then the 102 Brigade sustains the combat force when it deploys into the desert.

Since January 2024, 7 Light Mechanised Brigade has been NATO's

Very High Readiness Joint Task Force (Land) (VJTF(L)), and it has been on standby to operate across Europe at short notice. Logistics planners for 102 Brigade have been working with their NATO partners to co-ordinate the deployment and sustainment of the VJTF(L).

102 Brigade is heavily dependent on the Army Reserve to fill out its order of battle. It has one regular Royal Logistic Corps (RLC) Regiment, which contains both transport and supply chain capabilities. Repair of vehicles and equipment is provided by 2 Battalion, Royal Mechanical & Electrical Engineers (REME). These regular units are partnered with

three reserve RLC regiments and an Army Reserve REME battalion. Two of the Army Reserve RLC units have a transport role, and one has the role of providing fuel for Army Air Corps and Royal Air Force helicopters.

When the UK launched Operation Interflex to train Ukrainian troops in Britain in 2022, 102 Brigade had an important role to play. It organised the movement of the Eastern Europeans to training areas around Britain and provided uniforms, weapons, and equipment to the guests. The Ukrainians needed a vast amount of live ammunition during their training and 102 Brigade had to organise its delivery to firing ranges.

102 Operational Sustainment Brigade	
Headquarters	Prince William of Gloucester Barracks, Grantham
Force Logistic Regiment	
7 Regt RLC	Kendrew Barracks, Cottesmore
Transport Regiment (Army Reserve)	
150 Regiment RLC	Hull
158 Regiment RLC	Peterborough
159 Regiment RLC	Coventry
Repair Battalions	
2 (Force Support) Battalion REME	Leuchars Station
101 (Force Support) Battalion REME (Army Reserve)	Keynsham

LEFT: Chefs from the Royal Logistic Corps feed the British Army, wherever in the world it is deployed. (MOD/CROWN COPYRIGHT)

BELOW: Giant Oshkosh fuel tankers are used to refuel Army Air Corps helicopters at forward arming and refuelling points. (MOD/CROWN COPYRIGHT)

Army Special Operations Brigade

Rangers Deploy

To counter so-called hybrid threats in situations short of all-out war, the British Army has formed a unique regiment to specialise in operations in what has become known as the 'Grey Zone'.

The Rangers were formed by the then Chief of the General Staff Sir Mark Carleton-Smith to lead the fight against 'malign actors' by mobilising and leading local forces to turn back the tide of global instability.

In December 2021, the Ranger Regiment stood up and it took under its command the four specialist infantry battalions that previously had the role of training and advising allied armies or friendly militia groups.

Each of the Ranger Regiment's four battalions has a dedicated area of responsibility so personnel can build up language skills, local knowledge, and contacts with key local decision makers.

The Ranger Regiment is assigned to the Army Special Operations Brigade, which was specially formed in August 2021 to take the lead on training partner nations, but also fights alongside them. Its capabilities are akin to US 'Tier 2' special operations forces (SOF), which are built around the US Army's Special Forces or Green Berets.

As well as the Ranger Regiment, the brigade also has two reinforcement companies of the Royal Gurkha Rifles, along with 255 Signal Squadron under command and Army Reservists from 1 Squadron Honourable Artillery Company are attached to provide long range surveillance patrols.

The SOF Brigade also contains the Joint Counter Terrorist Training and Advisory Team (JCTTAT), which is configured to engage with partner armies counter-terrorist units. According to the British Army, the Ranger battalions and JCTTAT are optimised to operate alongside selected specialised partner forces in complex, high threat environments to counter threats posed by violent extremist organisations (VEO).

ABOVE: A new suite of uniforms and weapons has been bought to equip the Ranger battalions for their demanding role. (MOD/CROWN COPYRIGHT)

RIGHT: Ranger units wear a distinctive light grey beret. (MOD/CROWN COPYRIGHT)

For its unique role, SOF Brigade units are to be re-equipped with new weapons, uniforms, and other kit, under the Army Special Operations, Light Forces and Individual Combat Lethality and Protection project. This is budgeted at between £600m and £800m, according to the Ministry of Defence's Land Industrial Strategy. Over the next four years around £120m will be spent on equipment for the Ranger Regiment alone.

The first phase of this project involves the purchase of what is called the Alternative Individual Weapon (AIW) System. In tender documents issued to 16 international companies, this is to be a variant of the proven US 5.56mm calibre Armalite rifle. This is required to have signature reduction systems and optics for close quarter battle, as well as a blank firing system. More than 1,000 weapons are required to equip the four Ranger battalions and delivery of the first rifles commenced in August 2022.

The Rangers are also looking to replace their standard issue UK Multi Terrain Pattern or MPT camouflage uniforms. The CryeMultiCam combat shirts and trousers have already been trialled by the Rangers and a bigger order is now expected.

The Ranger Regiment was at the DSEI exhibition in September 2023 showing off its capabilities and explaining its role in defence engagement around the world. Several Rangers could be seen around the halls wearing their distinctive grey berets and peregrine falcon cap badge.

Since the regiment's formation, Ranger personnel have deployed in several countries in the Middle East and Africa, as well as training

Army Special Operations Brigade	
Headquarters	Saint Omer Barracks, Aldershot
Ranger Battalion	
1st Battalion, Ranger Regiment	Palace Barracks, Lisburn
2nd Battalion, Ranger Regiment	Keogh Barracks, Ash Vale
3nd Battalion, Ranger Regiment	Elizabeth Barracks, Pirbright
4th Battalion, Ranger Regiment	Normandy Barracks, Aldershot
Attached Gurkha Company	
G (Coriano) Company (ex 3 RGR)	Normandy Barracks, Aldershot
F (Falklands) Company (ex 3 RGR)	Keogh Barracks, Ash Vale
Support Units	
255 Signals Squadron	Swinton Barracks, Pernham Down
1 Squadron, Honourable Artillery Company (Army Reserve)	City of London

the Ukrainian army on British supplied anti-tank weapons in the days before the Russian invasion in February 2022.

The Ranger Regiment is now well on its way to becoming one of the British Army's busiest regiments. Teams of Rangers have been on the ground in some very unstable and dangerous places. During 2023, the 1st Battalion has been to Cameroon

ABOVE: The Ranger Regiment has adopted the peregrine falcon as its cap badge, because it is 'fast, agile, and fiercely loyal to its partner, it operates around the world in all environments including deserts, mountains, and cities'. (MOD/CROWN COPYRIGHT)

LEFT: The 3rd Ranger Battalion has the mission of operating in Europe, including the High North of Scandinavia. (MOD/CROWN COPYRIGHT)

LEFT: The Ranger Regiment is equipped with an array of non-standard weapons, including variants of the US-made AR-15 assault rifle. (MOD/CROWN COPYRIGHT)

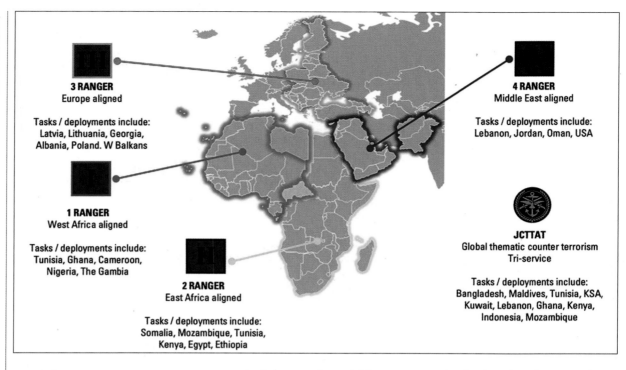

3 RANGER
Europe aligned

Tasks / deployments include:
Latvia, Lithuania, Georgia,
Albania, Poland. W Balkans

1 RANGER
West Africa aligned

Tasks / deployments include:
Tunisia, Ghana, Cameroon,
Nigeria, The Gambia

2 RANGER
East Africa aligned

Tasks / deployments include:
Somalia, Mozambique, Tunisia,
Kenya, Egypt, Ethiopia

4 RANGER
Middle East aligned

Tasks / deployments include:
Lebanon, Jordan, Oman, USA

JCTTAT
Global thematic counter terrorism
Tri-service

Tasks / deployments include:
Bangladesh, Maldives, Tunisia, KSA,
Kuwait, Lebanon, Ghana, Kenya,
Indonesia, Mozambique

6 (UK) Division

The Army Special Operations Brigade is assigned to 6 (UK) Division, which was re-organised in 2022 and 2023 to turn it into a formation specialising in asymmetric operations in Europe and further afield.

As well as the SOF Brigade, it controls the British Army's strategic influence organisation, 77 Brigade.

to train the country's special forces and the 4th Battalion spent time in the Middle East hotspot of Lebanon building up its ranger and special forces units.

Instability in East Africa has generated plenty for work for the 2nd Battalion, with a 73 strong contingent deploying to war-torn Somalia, where government forces and African Union troops are fighting Al Shabaab extremists. Another of its team has headed to

Mozambique, which has recently been rocked by an Islamic extremist insurgency.

Although the Rangers were originally formed from four infantry battalions they are now recruiting from across the British Army, with more than 50% of its personnel drawn of non-infantry regiments or corps. Prospective recruits undergo a selection process and those who are successful, undergo specialist training in Ranger skills.

77 Brigade

Winning the Information War

Modern conflicts are often won or lost because of control of the media narrative. For many years this was often a 'Cinderella' activity, carried out by British Army officers and soldiers assigned to be press officers for specific operations. These were 'gifted amateurs' who often had to build effective information campaigns without much guidance or resources.

During the Cold War, the British Army's information expertise resided in the Territorial Army Pool of Information Officers - the TAPIO - and from 1998 it became the Media Operations Group. These reservists were mobilised to support major operations.

From 2015, the Army Reservists of the Media Operations Group were combined with regular army experts into a new formation, dubbed 77 Brigade. This took its name and traditions from the World War Two Chindits, who operated behind Japanese lines in Burma. It is currently based at Denison Barracks in Hermitage, Berkshire but is due to move to a new site in Pirbright by 2026.

LEFT: 77 Brigade has adopted the badge and traditions of the World War Two Chindits, who fought behind enemy lines in Burma. (MOD/CROWN COPYRIGHT)

The brigade currently has regular, reserve, and civilian personnel assigned to it, including experts from the Foreign, Commonwealth and Development Office, as well as the Cabinet Office. It is a hybrid unit of regulars, reservists, and civilians with specialist skills to combat new forms of warfare in the information environment for the defence of the UK and its overseas territories.

To execute its mission, the brigade is organised into three main groups, which build capacity, deploy to operational theatres, and conduct stand-off activities. Information of overseas crisis zones is provided by 6 Military Intelligence Battalion and reservists from Honourable Artillery Company.

BELOW: Personnel of 77 Brigade deploy around the world in small teams to provide specialist information support to British forces. (MOD/CROWN COPYRIGHT)

ARRC

NATO's Reserve Force

The British Army's three-star headquarters, the Allied Rapid Reaction Corps (ARRC), is based at Innsworth, and stands ready to deploy to Europe and beyond on a variety of missions.

It is assigned to NATO as one of the alliance's reserve headquarters, which is at the disposal of the Supreme Allied Commander Europe (SACEUR) in time of crisis. A British lieutenant general leads the headquarters, and its staff of 200 British personnel are augmented by personnel from 20 NATO nations.

The headquarters is configured to allow it to operate as a corps headquarters, a land force component command, a joint task force headquarters, or to augment ongoing operations with select staff capabilities.

It was formed in 1992 from the old 1 (British) Corps headquarters and then was in the forefront of NATO operations in the Balkans and Afghanistan. The British-led headquarters led NATO peacekeeping forces into Bosnia in 1995-96 and Kosovo in 1999. When the US handed over command of its military mission to NATO in Afghanistan in 2006, the ARRC headquarters was given the mission of running allied operations in the central Asian country.

From 2023, the British government offered the ARRC to NATO to act as a reserve headquarters in case of a major war in Europe, under NATO's New Force Model.

1 Signals Brigade

Talking to the World

To support the ARRC headquarters wherever it deploys in the world, 1 Signals Brigade has two dedicated signals regiments to provide communications. These Stafford-based regiments operate satellite communications and supporting computer networks to allow senior ARRC staff to link up with their subordinate units and other allied headquarters. Two reserve signals regiments are assigned to augment their regular counterparts.

The Gurkha ARRC Support Battalion is based at Innsworth to provide security and force protection for the headquarters when it deploys to operational theatres.

Each year, the ARRC headquarters carries out a major exercise to test its ability to deploy around Europe and establish communication links to allied forces. This involves the movement of hundreds of vehicles and communication equipment to a remote location to set up a field headquarters, including the setting up of fortifications to protect it from attack.

1 Signals Brigade	
Headquarters	Imjin Barracks, Innsworth
Communications Units	
10 (ICS) Signals Regiment	Basil Hill Barracks, Corsham
16 Signals Regiment	Beacon Barracks, Stafford
22 (ARRC) Signals Regiment	Beacon Barracks, Stafford
30 Signals Regiment	Gamecock Barracks, Nuneton
32 Signals Regiment (Army Reserve)	Glasgow
39 Signals Regiment (Army Reserve)	Bristol
299 Signals Squadron	Bletchley
Logistics & Force Protection	
Gurkha ARRC Support Bn	Imjin Barracks, Innsworth

1 Signals Brigade also has a national role, supporting British operations around the world and allowing Permanent Joint Headquarters (PJHQ) to communicate with deployed forces by satellite. Small contingents of 30 Signals Regiment are held at a few hours notice to accompany the planners of the Joint Force Headquarters which is Britain's emergency response organisation.

The brigade also controls a unique unit, 299 Signals Squadron, which provides special communications support around the world to other departments of the British government.

LEFT: Royal Signals experts keep the communications network of ARRC Headquarters up and running. (MOD/CROWN COPYRIGHT)

LEFT: Tactical satellite communications terminals allow small troops detachments to feed information to ARRC Headquarters. (MOD/CROWN COPYRIGHT)

104 Theatre Sustainment Brigade

Moving the Army

ABOVE: Logistic experts from 17 Port & Maritime Regiment RLC were on hand in the Albanian port of Durres to receive troops of the Princess of Wales Royal Regiment to support NATO forces in Kosovo.
(MOD/CROWN COPYRIGHT)

Since 2019, the British Army has been almost entirely based in the United Kingdom, so it is dependent on units of the Royal Logistic Corps (RLC) to launch it on overseas operations.

The activation and sustainment of strategic lines of communications is the mission of 104 Theatre Sustainment Brigade, headquartered at South Cerney in Gloucestershire. Its nine major units are configured to co-ordinate air, land, and sea supply routes on a global scale. 104 Brigade is a unique formation and is central to all overseas British military operations.

In military jargon, 104 Brigade has a theatre entry role and its personnel are often the first British forces to arrive in new operational theatres. As a result, the brigade commander and his headquarters usually take on the role of National Support Element, providing a link back to Britain's

Permanent Joint Headquarters, until the main fighting formations are fully established in theatre and ready to begin operations.

From its base at Marchwood Military Port, 17 Port & Maritime

(P&M) Regiment loads vehicles and cargo onto military and commercial shipping. It also dispatches teams of experts to overseas ports to receive consignments of vehicles and cargoes for British forces. The regiment has

RIGHT: Marchwood Military Port in Hampshire is the home of 17 Port & Maritime Regiment RLC and the launching point of British overseas operations.
(MOD/CROWN COPYRIGHT)

104 Theatre Sustainment Brigade	
Headquarters	William of Gloucester Barracks, South Cerney
2 Operational Support Group RLC	Grantham
Port & Maritime Regiment	
17 P& M Regiment RLC	McMullen Barracks, Marchwood
165 P& M Regiment RLC (Army Reserve)	Plymouth
Movement Control Regiment	
29 PC&M Regiment RLC	Duke of Gloucester Barracks, South Cerney
162 PC&M Regiment RLC (Army Reserve)	Nottingham
Catering Support	
167 Regiment RLC (Army Reserve)	Grantham
Theatre Support Regiment	
9 Supply Regiment RLC	Buckley Barracks, Hullavington
151 (Fuel Support) Logistic Regiment RLC (Army Reserve)	Belfast
Repair Unit	
9 (Theatre Support) Battalion REME	New Normandy Barracks, Aldershot

watercraft and Mexeflote pontoons to bring vehicles and cargo ashore from vessels on to beaches. Army Reservists from its partner unit, 165 P&M Regiment can augment its operations.

The preparation of troops and cargo for movement by air is the responsibility of 29 Postal Courier and Movement Regiment at South Cerney, where it runs the Joint Air Mounting Centre (JAMC). Units heading for overseas deployment via nearby RAF Brize Norton are processed at the JAMC before being embarked on transport aircraft. It also dispatches personnel to overseas airfields to receive inbound units. Army Reservists from 162 Logistic Regiment RLC augments the unit.

The brigade is configured to establish Joint Support Areas (JSA) in operational theatres, where bulk fuel, ammunition and other supplies will be received and stockpiled before they are collected by operational sustainment brigades for delivery to frontline units.

It has theatre support, fuel supply and logistic operations RLC regiments that have the job of setting up and running the JSA. A Royal Electrical & Mechanical Engineer battalion keeps 104 Brigade's equipment working. Specialists in the brigade are responsible for contracting British and European railway companies to move British troops and equipment by train to Eastern Europe in support of NATO.

Part of the JSA is the establishment of reception camps to allowing arriving units to unpack their equipment and prepare to go into action. Feeding the troops in these camps is the job of reservist catering staff of 167 Regiment RLC.

104 Brigade keeps elements at high readiness to deploy on short notice deployments and a package of capabilities is brought together under the Vanguard Enabling Group. The group contains transport, movement control, port operations, catering, fuel handling, local contracting, equipment repair and ammunition handling expertise, as well as Royal Engineers, Royal Signals, and Royal Army Medical Corps detachments. First elements of this group are expected to be on the ground in overseas theatres to begin receiving contingents of British troops within a few days of a decision to commence operations.

LEFT: Feeding troops in reception camps in new theatres of operation is a key task of **104 Theatre Sustainment Brigade.** (MOD/CROWN COPYRIGHT)

BELOW: Mexeflote pontoons are used to bring vehicles and cargo ashore when established ports are not available. (MOD/CROWN COPYRIGHT)

1 Aviation Brigade Combat Team

Tip of the Spear

ABOVE: Army Air Corps Apache crews have trained to operate in the High North of Norway during major NATO exercises. (MOD/CROWNCOPYRIGHT)

The fighting units of the Army Air Corps are grouped together under 1 Aviation Brigade Combat Team (1 Avn BCT). It is a deployable headquarters that can bring together attack, reconnaissance, and transport helicopters into a single force to operate in a wide range of scenarios, from humanitarian and counter-insurgency operations through to peer-on-peer war fighting.

At its home bases, 1 Avn BCT reports to the tri-service Joint Aviation Command (JAC) but on operations it can be assigned to work under British Army, or allied, division or corps level headquarters.

1 Aviation Brigade first formed at Middle Wallop in April 2020 and was immediately involved in the British Army's response to the COVID-19 pandemic, flying personnel and medical supplies to support the National Health Service and other emergency services. It was formally redesignated to 1 Aviation Brigade Combat Team in October 2022 and

RIGHT: The AH-64E Apache provides the Army Air Corps' airborne firepower. (MOD/CROWNCOPYRIGHT)

achieved full operating capability in April 2023.

Its 800-strong Brigade Support Group provides essential maintenance and logistic support to sustain its helicopters on operations in all environments, from the Arctic to deserts and jungles. Helicopter maintenance is carried out by 7 Aviation Support Battalion Royal Electrical and Mechanical Engineers

Royal Logistic Corps personnel drive fuel and supply trucks, as well as running field kitchens, and moving spare parts and ammunition to forward operating bases. Regulars from 132 Aviation Supply Squadron RLC and reservists from 158 Regiment RLC are assigned to support the brigade.

The first AAC unit to fly the new Boeing AH-64E Apache attack

1 Combat Aviation Brigade	
Headquarters	Army Aviation Centre, Middle Wallop
Attack Helicopter Regiments (AH-64E)	
3 Regiment AAC	Wattisham Flying Station
4 Regiment AAC	Wattisham Flying Station
Reconnaissance Regiment (Wildcat AH1)	
1 Regiment AAC	RNAS Yeovilton
5 Regiment ACC (re-roling)	Aldergrove Flying Station
Support Group	
6 Regiment AAC (Army Reserve	Bury St Edmunds
7 (Aviation Close Support) Battalion REME	Wattisham Flying Station

The other operational attack helicopter unit based at Wattisham is 4 Regiment AAC. Up to the end of March 2024, it flew the legacy Apache AH1. These old helicopters have now been withdrawn from service to allow the regiment's squadrons to complete the conversion to the new AH-64E.

4 Regiment has taken on many innovative roles, including for the first-time flying combat missions from the Royal Navy flat top helicopter carrier, HMS *Ocean*, during the NATO-led air intervention in Libya in May 2011. For four »

LEFT: In May 2024, the AAC's new AH-64E attack helicopters joined exercises in Estonia for the first time. (MOD/CROWNCOPYRIGHT)

BELOW: AAC Apache and RAF Chinook helicopters joined forces to fly air assault missions during Exercise Swift Response in Estonia in May 2024. (MOD/CROWNCOPYRIGHT)

helicopter, 3 Regiment AAC, was declared ready for frontline duty at the end of 2023.

3 Regiment AAC achieved this important milestone after successfully participating in Exercise Iron Titan in October 2023. Across six weeks, 3 Regiment AAC deployed from its base at Wattisham Flying Station in Suffolk to set up temporary facilities at Nesscliffe in Shropshire, and then moved down to Eaglescott and Chivenor in Devon. Strike missions by the AH-64Es were planned and executed on simulated enemy positions as far apart as Otterburn in Northumberland and Lydd in Kent.

Throughout the exercise, REME technicians kept the aircraft in working order, while ground crew ran isolated Forward Arming and Refuelling Points - the military equivalent of a Formula 1 pit stop - to keep the aircraft's fuel tanks and weapons pylons full.

The AH-64E entered service in 2021 to replace the AgustaWestland Apache AH1, which had been in AAC service since 2004 and saw combat service in Afghanistan and Libya. Fifty of the new AH-64Es are on order, with just under 40 being delivered to Wattisham by the end of 2023. Several are also based at Middle Wallop for air and ground crew conversion training.

RIGHT: RAF Chinooks work as part of a single aviation task force headquarters alongside AAC helicopters when they assigned to 16 Air Assault Brigade.
(MOD/CROWNCOPYRIGHT)

BELOW: Field operating sites are the established by AAC regiments and supporting units to allow them to support army units as they manoeuvre around the battlefield.
(MOD/CROWNCOPYRIGHT)

Boeing AH-64E Attack Helicopter

In service:	2022 onwards
Used by:	British Army and 11 other air arms
Manufacturer:	Boeing
Produced:	2015 to 2025 for AAC
Number built:	50 to be built for the AAC

Specifications

Crew:	Two
Length:	48.16ft (14.68m)
Height:	15.49ft (4.72m)
Engine:	T700-GE-701D engines
Maximum level flight speed:	150+kts (279+kph)

Armament

Guns:	M230 Chain Gun, 1,200 rounds
Missiles:	8 × Hellfire laser guided
Rockets:	CRV7 with Flechette (Tungsten dart) or High-Explosive Incendiary Semi-Armour Piercing (HEISAP) warheads

months, the Apaches of 656 Squadron launched missions from the ship, as part of an Anglo-French attack helicopter operation. This was the first, and only time, UK Apaches have flown from warships during combat operations. The mission was judged a success, and the tactic is now routinely practiced in training, including from the new Queen Elizabeth-class aircraft carriers. This role is be continued by the AH-64E.

4 Regiment AAC took on the bulk of Apache operations tasking whilst its sister unit, 3 Regiment AAC, converted to the new AH-64E variant, including deploying on a short notice to Eastern Europe in response to the Russian invasion of Ukraine in February 2022.

The Army Air Corps' next most numerous rotary wing aircraft is the Leonardo Wildcat AH1 utility and battlefield surveillance helicopter.

It is the latest variant of the classic Lynx, which first entered service in the 1970s. The Lynx was developed as part of an Anglo-French initiative with the Yeovil-based Westland Helicopters leading the project. The Yeovil manufacturer is now part of the Italian aerospace company, Leonardo.

Work on the replacement for the Lynx started early this century and the UK eventually decided on buying specialist land and maritime variants. The land variant, the AH1, was less well equipped than the Royal Navy variant, the HMA2, which features a Sea Spray radar and is cleared to fire a variety of air-to-surface missiles. On land variant, the main sensor is a L-3 Wescam MX-15 HDi electro-optical/infrared camera, mounted in a nose turret. There have been proposals to fit the helicopter with an overland radar, data links, and missiles but none have yet been

LEFT: All the British Army's Wildcat AH1s are operated by 1 Regiment AAC and they regularly deploy to field locations. (MOD/CROWNCOPYRIGHT)

LEFT: Army Air Corps Wildcat AH1s can be armed with 0.50 cal machine guns. (MOD/CROWNCOPYRIGHT)

flying teams of experts and high value cargo around the United Kingdom to support the National Health Service.

In 2018, 1 Regiment AAC began deploying detachments of Wildcats to the Baltic states to support NATO's enhanced forward presence battle groups. The size and frequency of these deployments have progressively increased. They now regularly take their place as part of a joint aviation task force with AAC Apaches. Over the summer of 2023, 661 Squadron AAC spent four months in Estonia as part of the Aviation Task Force 1 (ATF-1) deployment to bolster NATO forces in the region.

approved. The only armament of the land variant are .50 cal door-mounted machine guns.

All the AAC Wildcats are operated by 1 Regiment AAC. It was originally formed at Hildesheim in Germany in January 1983, as the divisional anti-tank aviation regiment of 1 (UK) Armoured Division. It moved to Gutersloh in 1993, when it was still equipped with both the Lynx and Gazelle and remained as the sole AAC regiment based in Germany. The legacy Lynx AH7 and AH9 were progressively replaced by 34 upgraded Wildcat AH1 from 2015 onwards. These new helicopters were concentrated in a single unit, 1 Regiment AAC, based at RNAS Yeovilton in Somerset in 2015, alongside Wildcat AH1s operated by 847 Naval Air Squadron (NAS). All maintenance and training for both the

AAC and Royal Navy is carried out in shared facilities at Yeovilton.

Since then, all the land variants of the Wildcat have been operated as a single fleet, or pool, that is shared by 1 Regiment AAC and 847 NAS.

The AAC only has two operational Wildcat sub-units, 661 and 659 Squadrons, and 652 Squadron is the training/conversion sub-unit for the land variant.

The formation of the 1 Aviation Brigade meant the Wildcats were placed in this organisation, alongside the AAC's Boeing AH64E Apache attack helicopters. A pair of Wildcats are held at high readiness at Yeovilton to support national emergency operations around the UK.

The regiment played an important role during the initial phase of the COVID-19 pandemic in 2020,

Wildcat AH1 Battlefield Helicopter	
In service:	2014–present
Used by:	British Army and Royal Navy
Manufacturer:	AgustaWestland, now Leonardo
Produced:	2006 to 2016
Number built:	34 in use by the British Army and Royal Navy
Specifications	
Crew:	Two pilots
Capacity:	Six passengers, including door gunner
Length:	15.24m (50ft)
Height:	3.73m (12ft 3in)
Max take-off weight:	6,000kg (13,228lb)
Powerplant:	Two × LHTEC CTS800-4N turboshaft
Maximum speed:	311kph (193mph, 168kts)
Range:	777km (483 miles, 420nm)
Armament:	Pintle-mounted machine gun, e.g. GPMG (army)

Drone Warriors

Watching the Battlefield

modern version of their pilot wings in its insignia.

In September 2019, 47 Regiment RA changed from their black Royal Artillery headdress to that of the light blue Army Air Corps beret, although they retained their Gunner cap badge. This marked the regiment's transfer to the Joint Helicopter Command (JHC).

December 2023 saw the creation within JHC of a new Uncrewed Aircraft Systems (UAS) Group and the transfer of 32 Regiment RA to the new organisation. This group is intended to speed up the development, procurement, and employment of drones across the British Army. In April 2024, JHC became Joint Aviation

ABOVE: Watchkeeper pilot training is undertaken at Fort Bliss in the United States to give students access to a large area of military airspace and good weather. (MOD/CROWNCOPYRIGHT)

RIGHT: The Watchkeeper unmanned aerial vehicle provides army commanders with tactical intelligence. (MOD/CROWNCOPYRIGHT)

BELOW: 47 Regiment RA took its Watchkeepers to Oman in October 2023 to conduct a joint training exercise with 3 Regiment AAC's AH-64E Apaches. (MOD/CROWNCOPYRIGHT)

The Royal Artillery operates the British Army's uncrewed aerial vehicles/systems (UAS), and it currently has two regiments equipped with this important technology. These are universally known as 'drones'. Large tactical systems are operated by 47 Regiment RA and small, mini-drones are the responsibility of 32 Regiment RA.

The Royal Artillery has operated drones since the 1960s and but is now rapidly fielding new and more capable systems, as well as upgrading its existing platforms. Royal Artillery drone crews have adopted the traditions of the Royal Artillery Air Observation Post pilots from World War Two era, including a

Uncrewed Aerial Systems Group	
Headquarters	Larkhill
Tactical UAV Regiment (Watchkeeper)	
47 Regiment RA	Horne Barracks, Larkhill
Mini UAV Regiment	
32 Regiment RA	Roberts Barracks, Larkhill

Command as part of a drive to enhance the importance of UAS.

The Royal Artillery's UAS Group is concentrated on Salisbury Plain within the Larkhill Garrison complex. The Thales Watchkeeper WK450 is operated by 47 Regiment RA from its base at Larkhill. Local flying is conducted from the Ministry of Defence's Boscombe Down airfield and pilot training has taken place since 2022 at Fort Bliss in the United States, where the good weather and clear airspace allows for uninterrupted flying. Test and evaluation flying is conducted from QinetiQ's airfield at Aberporth in west Wales.

The Watchkeeper is undergoing a mid-life extension improvement project that will come online in 2026. The key elements of the upgrade will be to the ground control station, through an updated operating system, including wider systems integration. Obsolescence management appears to have a greater priority than adding new sensors or weapons to the air vehicle.

In the summer of 2020, 47 Regiment RA was deployed on its first operational missions to monitor the English Channel for boats carrying migrants towards Dover from France. A forward operating location was set up at Lydd Airport for the patrols over the Channel, under the codename Operation Deveran.

32 Regiment RA is the focus of British Army mini-drone developments. It is currently equipped with the US-made RQ-20 Puma and Wasp III mini-UAVs. In 2023, it was announced that 250 more advanced

Watchkeeper WK450 Tactical Unmanned Aerial Vehicle	
In service:	2014 to present
Used by:	British Army
Manufacturer:	UAV Tactical Systems (U-TacS) joint venture of Elbit Systems and the Thales group
Produced:	2005 to date
Number built:	54 air vehicles built
Specifications	
Length:	6.5m (21ft 3in)
Wingspan:	10.9m (35ft 7in)
Powerplant:	Single UAV Engines Limited R802/902(W) Wankel engine
Range from ground station:	150km (93 miles)
Cruise speed:	142kph (88mph, 77kts)
Altitude:	4,876m (16,000ft)
Aircraft endurance:	14 hours

systems, including 159 rotary-wing Indago 4 devices, and 105 fixed-wing Stalker VXE30 drones, would be purchased for the regiment under Project Tiquila. Ahead of the arrival of the new systems later this year an additional battery was formed within the regiment in December 2023. They operate from FV432 Bulldog tracked armoured vehicles to provide drone support to armoured units.

Small detachments of mini-UAVs from 32 Regiment RA are routinely assigned to operate with British Army infantry and armoured battlegroups on training grounds around the UK and overseas.

LEFT: Royal Artillery crews download live video imagery from Puma mini-drones into small terminals that can be carried in back packs. (MOD/CROWNCOPYRIGHT)

BELOW: 32 Regiment RA operates the British Army's Puma mini-drones and provides small detachments to support infantry and armoured units. (MOD/CROWNCOPYRIGHT)

2 Medical Group

Battlefield Medics

ABOVE: Field hospitals in forward areas are tasked with stabilising casualties before they can be evacuated back to Britain.
(MOD/CROWN COPYRIGHT)

The British Army's medical services have come a long way since the days of Florence Nightingale and the Crimean War, when wounded soldiers suffered terribly from a cholera epidemic, insanitary conditions, and lack of supplies.

Since its formation in 1898, the Royal Army Medical Corps (RAMC) has become one of the leading military medical organisations in the world. Survival rates for battlefield casualties in the Iraq and Afghanistan conflicts were far in excess of those in World War Two thanks to speedy evacuation and improved treatments.

The British Army now has a well-established doctrine to run its medical evacuation chain to ensure wounded soldiers are rapidly collected from the battlefield and moved back to medical facilities in Britain.

Frontline infantry, armoured, and artillery units have their own 'Role 1' medical teams to triage and treat casualties. These used to be called regimental aid posts or RAPs. Armoured ambulance units or medical evacuation helicopters, then move the casualties back to 'Role 2' field hospitals immediately behind the frontline where they are stabilised. Casualties are then

moved to theatre level 'Role 3' field hospitals where more complex surgery can be carried out. At these facilities, decisions can be made on whether casualties need to be evacuated back to major hospitals and rehabilitation centres in Britain. The majority of these 'Role 4' hospitals are run by the National Health Service, although some patients can be sent to the Defence Medical Rehabilitation Centre (DMRC) at Stanford Hall, which replaced Headley Court, where casualties from Iraq and Afghanistan were treated, in 2018.

The RAMC has been re-organised since 2021 to make it more flexible and allow a rotation of units to take place to sustain the provision of medical support during enduring campaigns. This has led to the transformation of old field hospital units into multi-role medical regiments (MMRs), which have the personnel and equipment to set up and sustain Role 2 and Role 3 hospitals, as well as operating the medical evacuation chain. From its headquarters at Strensall in North Yorkshire, 2 Medical Group controls the main British Army medical units, drawing personnel from the

RIGHT: Royal Army Medical Corps personnel are responsible for running the British Army's casualty evacuation chain.
(MOD/CROWN COPYRIGHT)

2 Medical Group	
Headquarters	Queen Elizabeth Barracks, Strensall
Multi-Role Medical Regiment (Regular)	
21 Multi-role Medical Regiment RAMC	Queen Elizabeth Barracks, Strensall
22 Multi-role Medical Regiment RAMC	Keogh Barracks, Aldershot
Multi-Role Medical Regiment (Army Reserve)	
214 (North East) Multi-role Medical Regiment RAMC	Newcastle/Sheffield
202 (Midlands) Multi-role Medical Regiment RAMC	Birmingham
203 (Welsh) Multi-role Medical Regiment RAMC	Cardiff
21 (North Irish) Multi-role Medical Regiment RAMC	Belfast
215 (Scottish) Multi-role Medical Regiment RAMC	Glasgow
206 (North West) Multi-role Medical Regiment RAMC	Manchester/Liverpool
243 (Wessex) Multi-role Medical Regiment RAMC	Keynsham
254 (East of England) Multi-role Medical Regiment RAMC	Cambridge
256 (London & South East) Multi-role Medical Regiment RAMC	Walworth
Specialist Units (Army Reserve)	
306 Hospital Support Regiment RAMC	Queen Elizabeth Barracks, Strensall
335 Medical Evacuation Regiment RAMC	Queen Elizabeth Barracks, Strensall
Medical Support Unit RAMC	Queen Elizabeth Barracks, Strensall

RAMC, Royal Army Dental Corps, and Queen Alexandra's Royal Army Nursing Corps.

There are two regular MMRs which are held at high readiness to deploy around the world and establish Role 2 and Role 3 hospitals. Each regiment is configured to support a brigade-sized deployment for a few months. For large scale operations or enduring campaigns, the RAMC will turn to its Army Reserve units, which are predominately made up of personnel who work full time in the National Health Service. There are nine Army Reserve MMRs that were formed out of the old field hospitals. Supporting them are three other reserve units that have specialist evacuation teams, hospital services, and medical support roles.

During the Iraq and Afghan wars, helicopters with a medical emergency response team (MERT) were the primary means of evacuating battlefield casualties to field hospitals.

In high intensity combat it might not be possible or safe to send helicopters into high threat areas, so the British Army is purchasing an armoured ambulance version of the Boxer vehicle. This will have the same equipment as a helicopter-borne MERT to allow badly wounded casualties to be kept alive until they reach a field hospital.

ABOVE: The bulk of RAMC personnel are reservists who work full time in the National Health Service, so are highly skilled in emergency and other forms of medicine. (MOD/CROWN COPYRIGHT)

LEFT: Medics from the Army Reserve are routinely tested on complex exercises so they can be rapidly mobilised in time of crisis or war. (MOD/CROWN COPYRIGHT)

Home Command

Regional Forces and MACA

Day-to-day command of soldiers and garrisons around Britain is the responsibility of Home Command, which is located in Montgomery House in Aldershot. It controls the main recruit training depots, recruiting offices, the Royal Military Academy Sandhurst, support for veterans, and the welfare of families of army personnel. It has a network of regional headquarters across Britain to co-ordinate its activities.

Military support to high profile public events is also co-ordinated by Home Command. When these involve the royal family, Headquarters London District in the iconic Horse Guards building, takes the lead.

The British Army has an important role to provide military assistance to civilian authorities in response to emergencies, natural disasters, and security incidents. These are known as MACA tasks and involve soldiers being dispatched to help local authorities, devolved administrations, the National Health Service, emergency services, and police forces.

These are often termed resilience operations and recent examples includes floods in the southwest and northwest of England in 2014 and 2016 respectively, the response to the foot and mouth outbreak in 2001, and the security mission for the 2012 London Olympics.

This is a semi-permanent role as these missions are continuously ongoing, with staff officers and liaison teams engaging with key players across the country. Since 2017, the British Army has provided specialist personnel and capabilities to support counterterrorist police operations across Britain, under the banner of Operation Temperer. A key part of 'Temperer' involved teams from the UK Special Forces Group but contingency plans for wider military involvement have been routinely activated. When armed police units found themselves under strain following a series of terrorist incidents in 2017, Operation Temperer was activated. This response saw hundreds of armed soldiers being mobilised to guard key military bases and nuclear power stations, to allow armed Ministry of Defence Police and British Nuclear Constabulary officers to be deployed on the streets of Britain. Some troops protected high profile buildings in central London. Royal Logistics Corps and Royal Engineer explosive ordnance disposal and search teams

are on continuous alert to support the police and emergency services.

The commander of Home Command is also designated the Standing Joint Commander UK (SJC(UK)) if a national scale resilience mission is ever required. In the days after the start of the COVID-19 pandemic in March 2020, the SJC (UK) Headquarters was activated to co-ordinate the military component of the national response to the crisis. At its peak in the summer and autumn of 2020, more than 23,000 personnel were taking part in Operation Rescript, as SJC (UK) Headquarters involvement in the pandemic was codenamed. It was dubbed the Covid

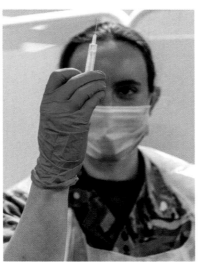

Home Command	
Headquarters	Montgomery House, Aldershot
38 (Irish) Brigade	Thiepval Barracks, Lisburn
160 (Welsh) Brigade	The Barracks, Brecon
Headquarters South West	Jellalabad Barracks, Tidworth
Headqaurters East	Kendrew Barracks, Cottesmore
Headqaurters South East	Taurus House, Aldershot
Headqaurters West Midlands	Vennings Barracks, Donnington
London District	Horse Guards, London
51 Infantry Brigade and HQ Scotland	Redford Barracks, Edinburgh
Balaklava Company, 5th Battalion, Royal Regiment of Scotland	Edinburgh Castle

Support Force and detachments of troops were deployed around Britain to carry out COVID-19 testing, drive ambulances, help run hospitals, and build the famous Nightingale hospitals.

As the pandemic escalated rapidly in 2020, SJC(UK) Headquarters developed contingency plans to deal with a possible breakdown in law and order, as well as possible mass casualties. Fortunately, it was not necessary to activate them.

In recent years, Home Command has also been involved in filling gaps left in public services during industrial disputes. Military personnel have operated fire engines, manned passport control points at airports, and driven fuel tankers.

LEFT: Military personnel were called in to kick start the test and trace effort during the COVID-19 pandemic. (MOD/CROWN COPYRIGHT)

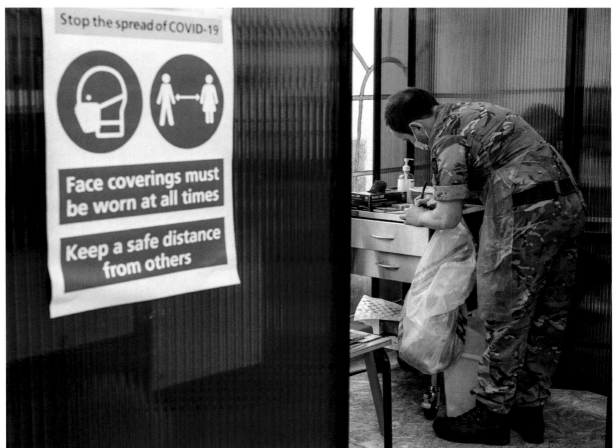

LEFT: The British Army was called up to help the National Health Service respond to the COVID-19 pandemic. (MOD/CROWN COPYRIGHT)

Training the Army

Getting Ready to Fight

RIGHT: British soldiers learn to fire the full range of infantry weapons during their basic training.
(MOD/CROWN COPYRIGHT)

The British Army is perpetually training - either passing the basic skills of soldiering to new recruits or honing the skills of those already in uniform. New recruits undergo their phase one, or 'boot camp' induction training at army training regiments at Pirbright, Winchester, and Grantham, as well as at the Infantry Training Centre at Catterick in Yorkshire.

Once they have learnt how to march and salute, use their personal equipment, fire their weapon, and live in the field, they move to phase two, or trade, training at their corps depot or specialist school. For infantry recruits, this means staying at Catterick to learn more advanced infantry combat skills. Soldiers from other arms and corps undergo training to repair tanks, fire artillery pieces, build bridges, or analyse intelligence.

BELOW: The British Army's officers are trained at the Royal Military Academy Sandhurst.
(MOD/CROWN COPYRIGHT)

Young officers follow a similar career progression after completing their initial training at the Royal Military Academy Sandhurst in Berkshire.

Throughout a soldier's career they undergo continuous training to prepare them for promotion or specialist roles. In the infantry, to be

promoted to corporal and sergeant, soldiers have to pass gruelling courses at the Infantry Battle School at Brecon in Wales. Each arm and corps run specialist technical courses at their depots to teach soldiers new skills.

Officers from across the army who are set for promotion have to attend the Joint Services Command and Staff College at Shrivenham in Oxfordshire.

Almost all of this training takes places on the British Army's extensive network of training areas and firing ranges. The largest is the Salisbury Plain training area in Wiltshire, which is close to most of the big garrisons and barracks. Other large ranges at Castlemartin in Wales and Otterburn in Northumberland are where live firing of tanks and artillery takes place. A dedicated facility, where large, battlegroup-sized armoured forces can manoeuvre and fire all their heavy weapons, has been set up at Sennelager in Germany. Similar facilities for light-role infantry battalions have been set up in Kenya and Oman. Tropical jungle training takes place in Belize in Central America and Brunei in the Far East.

ABOVE: British Army soldiers pass out from their phase one or basic training in a formal parade in front of their friends and families. (MOD/CROWN COPYRIGHT)

LEFT: Map reading is still a core military skill despite the proliferation of Google maps on mobile devices. (MOD/CROWN COPYRIGHT)

London District and Ceremonial

Bearskins and Parades

RIGHT: The public duties company of the Coldstream Guards is based full time at Wellington Barracks in London to support royal and state ceremonial events.
(MOD/CROWN COPYRIGHT)

Britain's red coated Guards are iconic because of their starring role at royal ceremonial events. This public role is a minor part of the duties of the British Army's Guards regiments, and they are routinely deployed around the world on operational tasks.

Ceremonial activities by the troops of the Household Division are co-ordinated by the Headquarters London District, which is based in the iconic Horse Guards building in Whitehall. It also has the task of co-ordinating with the Metropolitan Police and other civilian authorities in the capital in the event of major security incidents or emergencies.

The operational roles and missions of the Guards regiments have undergone major changes as a result of the 2021 Future Soldier plan to re-organise the British Army. This has seen the Guards receive new missions and equipment to deal with changing threats and defence requirements.

The Guards regiments are grouped into the Household Division for ceremonial duties and for routine peacetime administration. For operational tasks, Guards units are assigned to British Army brigades and divisions.

Household Cavalry Regiment (HCR)

The senior regiment of the Household Division is an integral part of the

BELOW: Coldstream Guards take part in a jungle training exercise in Malaysia.
(MOD/CROWN COPYRIGHT)

London District	
Headqurters	Horse Guards
1st Battalion, Welsh Guards	Combermere Barracks, Windsor
1st Battalion, London Guards (Army Reserve)	Battresea, London
Household Cavalry Mounted Regiment	Hyde Park Barracks, London
King's Troop, Royal Horse Artillery	Woolwich Barracks, London
Number 9 Company, Irish Guards	Wellington Barracks, London
Number 12 Company, Irish Guards,	Wellington Barracks, London
Nijmegen Company, Grenadier Guards	Wellington Barracks, London
Number 7 Company, Coldstream Guards	Wellington Barracks, London
F Company, Scots Guards	Wellington Barracks, London

The introduction of the Ajax has been plagued by technical problems and it was only declared safe to use earlier this year. Up to date, the HCR has received more than 30 Ajax vehicles and they have participated in a major army exercise on Salisbury Plain.

While the regiment waits to receive its full complement of Ajax vehicles. It recently deployed on United Nations Peacekeeping duties in Cyprus. Several HCR troopers were injured when rioting broke out along the UN administered ceasefire line. »

British Army's Royal Armoured Corps (RAC), which operate main battle tanks and armoured reconnaissance vehicles.

The HCR is currently based in Bulford on Salisbury Plain and is part of the 1 Deep Strike Recce Brigade, which combines RAC reconnaissance units with long range guns and rockets of the Royal Artillery.

To prepare it for this high-profile role, the HCR is in the process of re-equipping with the new Ajax family of armoured reconnaissance vehicles. These vehicles boast high levels of armoured protection and specialist surveillance equipment.

LEFT: The Duke of Edinburgh is the colonel-in-chief of the London Guards, the Army Reserve unit of the Household Division. (MOD/CROWN COPYRIGHT)

BELOW: Red coated Guardsmen are an important attraction for tourists visiting London. (MOD/CROWN COPYRIGHT)

Grenadier Guards

The 1st Battalion, Grenadier Guards are currently based in Aldershot and have a light role, operating as dismounted infantry as part of 4 Light Brigade Combat Team. They returned from Iraq in June 2023, after spending a year training and advising local forces as part of the continuing mission to contain the remnants of the so-called Islamic State (ISIS), under the banner Operation Shader.

Coldstream Guards

The 1st Battalion, Coldstream Guards is also a light role infantry unit based in Windsor and it serves alongside the Grenadier Guards

The Household Division

The regiments that form the Household Division have a long and proud history, mostly dating back to the time of the English Civil War and the Restoration in the middle of the 17th Century. Since that time, they have proudly carried out a dual role as the sovereign's personal troops and the nation's crack fighting soldiers.

The Brigade of Guards was initially made up of the Grenadier Guards, Coldstream Guards and Scots Guards. The Irish Guards was added to the Brigade in April 1900 at the wish of Queen Victoria to commemorate the bravery shown by the Irish regiments during the South African or Boer Wars.

In February 1915, a letter was published in *The Times* suggesting that a regiment of Welsh Guards should be added to the brigade and the unit was formed soon afterwards. In December 1950, the Household Cavalry joined with the Brigade of Guards to establish the Household Brigade, re-named the Household Division in July 1968.

In 1992, the two regiments of Household Cavalry – the Life Guards and Blues and Royals - were joined together to form the Household Cavalry Regiment, with armoured reconnaissance units based at Bulford, and the Household Cavalry Mounted Regiment, based at Hyde Park Barracks to carry out ceremonial duties.

Each foot regiment of the Household Division now has just one battalion, in addition to five public duties companies based at Wellington Barracks in London for ceremonial events:

- Number 9 Company, Irish Guards
- Number 12 Company, Irish Guards
- Nijmegen Company, Grenadier Guards
- Number 7 Company, Coldstream Guards
- F Company, Scots Guards

ABOVE: Troops of the Grenadier Guards serving on the Western Front in France in August 1918. (MOD/CROWN COPYRIGHT)

in 4 Light Brigade Combat Team. Over the past year its soldiers have deployed from their Windsor garrison on training exercises to Jamaica and Belize, as well as assisting in major ceremonial events in London. In October 2023, it undertook jungle warfare training with its Malaysian, Singaporean, Australian and New Zealand counterparts.

Scots Guards

From its base in Catterick, in North Yorkshire, 1st Battalion, Scots Guards operate as a heavy protected mobility unit, equipped with Mastiff mine protected vehicles and Jackal patrol vehicles. The battalion is part of 7 Light Mechanised Brigade Combat Team and has a conventional war fighting role. In 2022, the battalion's support weapons company was detached to serve with NATO forces in Estonia, practising to repel a Russian invasion with its Javelin anti-tank missiles and 81mm mortars. The battalion has the additional task of supporting the British garrison on Cyprus with two years in every six to be spent on the Mediterranean island.

Irish Guards

The 2021 Future Soldier plan gave the 1st Battalion, Irish Guards, a unique new role providing advice and training to allied forces around the world. It contains a higher proportion of officers and senior non-commissioned officers than in a traditional infantry battalion, to bring in personnel with specialist skills, including organising field firing exercises, advising local forces, and running a wide range of military training activities. The battalion is based in Aldershot.

Welsh Guards

The Windsor-based 1st Battalion, Welsh Guards are currently the

BRITISH ARMY YEARBOOK 2024

On Parade

The Changing the Guard ceremonies at Buckingham Palace and Windsor Castle attract large crowds of tourists, who want to lap up the tradition and watch the precision drills.

The Old Guard - the soldiers currently on duty - form up in front of the palace and are relieved by the New Guard, which arrives from Wellington Barracks. The New Guard is accompanied by a band. The ceremony represents a formal handover of responsibilities. The guard at Buckingham Palace is typically provided by one of the five foot guards regiments of the Household Division, but other units of the British Army, Royal Navy, and Royal Air Force also take their turn.

Changing of The King's Guard takes place in front of Buckingham Palace at 10:45am and lasts for about 45 minutes. Soldiers gather at St James's Palace and Wellington Barracks from 10am and march to Buckingham Palace accompanied by music.

When to see Changing of the Guard
• Buckingham Palace: Every Monday, Wednesday, Friday, and Sunday
• Windsor Castle: Every Tuesday, Thursday, and Saturday, at 11am

ABOVE: The pipe band of the Irish Guards on parade outside Buckingham Palace. (MOD/CROWN COPYRIGHT)

lead unit for what are termed State Ceremonial and Public Duties (SCPD), providing the bulk of troops for high profile events in London and Windsor, such as Trooping the Colour and visits for foreign heads of state. It will spend four years in this high profile before returning to operational tasks.

BELOW: Jackal patrol vehicles were used by Guards regiments on active service in Afghanistan. (MOD/CROWN COPYRIGHT)

Special Forces

Who Dares Wins and More

RIGHT: World War Two desert raiders – the classic special forces role.
(IMPERIAL WAR MUSEUM)

The famous Special Air Service (SAS) Regiment has a global reputation that is second to none among the world's special forces units. It was formed during World War Two to take the fight behind enemy lines in North Africa and has since seen almost continuous service on counterinsurgency, counterterrorist, and other operations that require its unique soldiers.

Over the past 20 years the UK Special Forces Group has grown into a significant organisation that involves units and more than 3,000 personnel from the British Army, Royal Marines, and Royal Air Force.

The army component of the special forces is mainly based at the home of the SAS at Stirling Lines in Credenhill, near Hereford. As well as the long-established 22 SAS Regiment, the base is home to the covert surveillance operatives

BELOW: The Special Forces Support Group stood up in 2004 to provide a unique capability to mount large scale raids and theatre entry operations.
(MOD/CROWN COPYRIGHT)

UK Special Forces Group	
Headquarters	Regent's Park, London
22 Special Air Service Regiment	Stirling Lines, Credenhill
Special Reconnaissance Regiment	Stirling Lines, Credenhill
1st Battalion, Parachute Regiment	RAF St Athan
Special Boat Service (RM)	RM Poole
18 (United Kingdom Special Forces) Signal Regiment	Stirling Lines, Credenhill
Joint Special Forces Aviation Wing	
7 Squadron, RAF	RAF Odiham
658 Squadron, AAC	Credenhill

of the Special Reconnaissance Regiment (SRS) and specialist communications experts of 18 Signals Regiment. A detachment of the Army Air Corps, assigned to 658 Squadron AAC, is also based at Stirling Lines to rapidly deploy personnel on counter-terrorist operations around the UK.

Since 2006, the Parachute Regiment has provided a battalion of its highly trained soldiers to serve in the Special Forces Support Group (SFSG), based at RAF St Athan in South Wales. This unit is akin to the US Army Rangers and is trained and equipped to mount large-scale raids behind enemy lines or to seize forward operating bases for other units of the Special Forces Group.

To serve in the SAS or SRS, soldiers have to undergo a gruelling selection and training process. Only a small fraction of the volunteers pass this and end up being 'badged' as fully fledged special forces operatives. There are two Army Reserve SAS units, 21 SAS (Artists Rifles) and 23 SAS Regiments, and potential recruits have to pass a version of the selection process to serve in them.

UK special forces are known to have been involved in almost every conflict involving the British armed forces over the past 30 years, from the 1991 Gulf War to the recent conflict against so-called Islamic State (ISIS) in Syria and Iraq. There is close co-operation between US, Australian, and other allied special forces units.

The SAS became famous after the 1980 Iranian Embassy rescue operation and since then the regiment and other elements of the Special Forces have provided specialist support to counter-terrorist police throughout the UK.

Special forces units are often equipped with specialist weapons, equipment, and vehicles for their unique role.

Most aspects of the UK Special Forces Group are classified, and the Ministry of Defence routinely declines to comment on their operations.

LEFT: In Afghanistan, the Special Forces Support Group operated in co-operation with the US Marines as part of Task Force 444. (US DOD/COMBAT CAMERA)

BELOW: The UK's special forces have their own squadron of Dauphin helicopter to transport them to counterterrorist incidents around the UK. (MARK HARKIN)

Global Army

On Watch

They used to say that the sun never set on the British Empire. In the 21st century the British Army no longer guards colonies around the world, but it has an important role protecting the last handful of overseas territories that remain and several important allies.

Consequently, the British Army still has a network of bases in the Far East, Middle East, Africa, Central America, the Caribbean, and the South Atlantic. In addition to deterring attacks on British overseas territories and responding to natural disasters, airbases and ports in these territories provide strategic jumping off points in time of crisis. Some also host strategic intelligence-gathering sites run by the GHCQ eavesdropping organisation. In the new jargon introduced in the 2021 Future Soldier plan these bases are 'regional hubs' that can be used to project military power, support diplomatic engagement, and help build trade relationships around the world.

There are now few permanent garrisons outside the United Kingdom so the British Army's presence around the world increasingly takes the form of

training deployments to show the flag and build relationships with host nation armed forces.

The largest permanent overseas British Army presence is in the Mediterranean, where two resident infantry battalions protect UK sovereign bases on the island of Cyprus. In addition to providing the ground defence of a major Royal Air Force airfield and the main GCHQ Middle East listening post, at least one of the battalions is kept at high readiness to deploy around the Middle East and Africa in time of crisis. At the other end of the Mediterranean, is the British overseas territory of Gibraltar. It is more than 30 years since there was a permanent infantry presence on 'the Rock' and now soldiers of the locally recruited Royal Gibraltar Regiment guard British military bases on the territory.

British Army soldiers have protected the Falkland Islands continuously since the defeat of Argentine occupation forces in the 1982 conflict. The burden of defending the islands falls on RAF Typhoons and Royal Navy warships but an infantry company and a battery of Royal Artillery surface-to-air-missiles have a key role securing Mount Pleasant Airport. These units rotate every four to six months from garrisons in the UK. The Royal Artillery replaced its veteran Rapier missiles with the new Sky Sabre system in 2021. Locally recruited troops of the Falkland Islands Defence Force

LEFT: The Royal Gibraltar Regiment provides the British military presence on 'the Rock', which dominates the entrance to the Mediterranean. (MOD/CROWN COPYRIGHT)

Permanent Joint Headquarters Units	
Headquarters	Northwood
British Forces Cyprus	Episkopi Station, Cyprus
1st Battalion, Duke of Lancaster's Regiment	Episkopi Station, Cyprus
1st Battalion, Rifles	Alexander Barracks, Dhekelia
Op Tosca (Rotation Battalion)	UN Buffer Zone
British Forces South Atlantic	Mount Pleasant Base, Falkland Islands
Roulement Infantry Company	Mount Pleasant Base, Falkland Islands
Roulement Air Defence Battery	Mount Pleasant Base, Falkland Islands
British Forces Gibraltar	Devil's Tower Camp
Royal Gibraltar Regiment	Devil's Tower Camp
British Forces Brunei	Tuker Lines, Brunei
1st Battalion, Royal Gurkha Rifles	Tuker Lines, Brunei
Trainings Units	
British Army Training Unit Kenya (BATUK)	Nanyuki, Kenya
British Army Training Support Unit Belize (BATSUB)	Price Barracks, Belize City
Omani-British Joint Training Area	Duqm, Oman
British Army Training Unit Suffield (BATUS)	Alberta, Canada

support personnel to the defence forces of overseas territories in the Caribbean, including the Royal Bermuda Regiment, the Cayman Regiment, the Turks and Caicos Regiment, and the Royal Montserrat Defence Force.

Facilities exist in Kenya to allow a full infantry battlegroup to conduct live-firing training. The British Army Training Unit Kenya (BATUK) also has a laser simulation facility so troops can conduct force-on-force training to enhance their tactical skills. The site is also used extensively to train troops from friendly African countries before they deploy on peacekeeping duties in Somalia and elsewhere.

Since 2019, the British Army has been expanding its training facilities in Oman, near the port of Duqm, setting up a training area where tanks and other armoured vehicles can exercise in desert conditions.

BELOW: Despite the Ukraine war, the British Army continues to invest in jungle training to ensure it is ready for unexpected conflicts. (MOD/CROWN COPYRIGHT)

are available to supplement the British garrison in a crisis.

The third major foreign garrison is in Brunei, where a battalion of Gurkha soldiers and RAF Eurocopter Puma HC2 helicopters help protect the sultanate and run jungle-training facilities.

A small contingent of soldiers is also based in the mountain kingdom of Nepal to run the recruiting process for Gurkha soldiers.

Another jungle-training facility is maintained in Central America. The British Army Training and Support Unit Belize has a small contingent of training staff who support units arriving from the UK. The British Army also provides training and administrative

Future Tech

RIGHT: The Boxer mechanised infantry vehicle is set to become the British Army's main combat vehicle.
(MOD/CROWN COPYRIGHT)

RIGHT: Exercises with robot dogs are part of a series of British Army experiments in future combat tactics.
(MOD/CROWN COPYRIGHT)

Drones, new artillery, improved rockets, and upgraded tanks are soon to be in the hands of soldiers as a £41bn programme to re-equip the British Army gathers momentum.

Boxer Mechanised Infantry Vehicle	
In service:	2024?
Used by:	Germany, Netherlands, Australia, Lithuania
Manufacturer:	Rheinmetall BAE Systems Land (RBSL)
Produced:	2021-2032
Number built:	623 on order
Specifications (baseline infantry section vehicle)	
Mass:	36.5 to 38.5 tonnes
Length:	7.93m (26ft)
Width:	2.99m (9ft 10in)
Height:	2.37m (7ft 9in) (baseline vehicle)
Crew:	In APC configuration – three plus, maximum of eight passengers
Armour:	AMAP composite armour
Main armament:	L94A1 coaxial 7.62mm chain gun, with Kongsberg Protector Remote Weapon Station
Engine:	MTU 8V199 TE20 Diesel
Operational range:	1,100km (684 miles)
Maximum speed:	103kph (64mph)

By the end of the decade almost every piece of British Army kit should have been replaced or upgraded as part of the service's biggest ever modernisation project.

The re-equipment project is part of the Future Soldier initiative that was launched in November 2021, with the ambition of making the British Army the 'most lethal in Europe'. The aim is to enable the British Army to take on and defeat so-called 'near peer adversaries' in high intensity combat. In other words, British soldiers will be able to go toe-to-toe with anything the Russians could send into action against NATO.

The modernisation efforts involve every aspect of the British Army – from helicopters, to tanks, artillery, small arms, bridges, and logistic vehicles.

Armoured forces of 3 (UK) Division are expected to get new tanks, reconnaissance vehicles, troop carriers, artillery, rockets, and engineering vehicles. These projects are all under contract with the first pieces of kit in the process of being delivered.

First to arrive are Boxer wheeled armoured personnel carriers, which

are set to begin replacing the veteran Warrior infantry fighting vehicles. The first two prototypes arrived in Britain from Germany last December to allow testing to take place, ahead of entry to service.

Archer Self-Propelled Gun	
In service:	2023
Used by:	British Army, Sweden, Ukraine
Manufacturer:	BAE Systems AB
Produced:	2010 - present
Number built:	14 for British Army
Specifications	
Chassis:	6×6 chassis Volvo A30D all-terrain articulated hauler
Mass:	34.0 tonnes
Length:	14.3m (47ft)
Width:	3m (9.8ft)
Height:	4m (13.1ft)
Crew:	1 driver, 1 commander, 2 operators
Armour:	Steel & appliqué armour
Main armament:	155mm
Ammunition:	Maxazine 21 rounds, including HE, M982 Excallibur guided rounds, BONUS, smoke, illumination and training rounds
Engine:	Volvo D9B AC E3 diesel,
Operational range:	650km (400 miles)
Maximum speed:	103kph (64mph)

The British Army is buying 623 Boxers in three/four main variants. These are the baseline protected mobility (PM) variant (MIV-PM), a command and control (MIV-CC), an ambulance (MIV-A), and a repair/recovery (MIV-REP) variant. While the first 117 vehicles are being built on German production lines, British facilities in Telford and Stockport are ramping up their manufacturing capabilities for the remaining 506.

The eight-wheeled Boxer is designed around a common chassis and cab. Its rear cabin can be rapidly fitted with new mission modules, depending on its specific role.

Britain's armoured fist is being modernised with the development of a new version of the Challenger main battle tank. Prototypes of the Challenger 3 are currently undergoing trials in Germany and the first tanks are expected to enter service by 2027.

This new version has a 120mm smooth-bore main armament, a new turret, new night-vision and fire control systems, improvements to the chassis, as well as the Israeli-made

Trophy countermeasures system to defeat enemy missiles and shells.

To create the new tanks, the hulls, and many other components from existing Challenger 2s are being recycled. Under current plans the Royal Armoured Corps is to receive 148 of the new tanks to equip the Queen's Royal Hussars and Royal Tank Regiment.

A major effort is underway to enhance the firepower available to the Royal Artillery. The Enhanced Range variant of the Guided Multiple Launch Rocket System (GMLRS) is being bought for the Royal Artillery and other variants of the rocket are under development.

The veteran AS90 155mm self-propelled howitzer is now set to be retired by early 2025 so the guns can be donated to Ukraine. As an interim measure, 14 Swedish-made Archer 155mm self-propelled guns are in the process of being brought into service and will deploy to Estonia next year. »

LEFT: The Swedish-made Archer 155mm self-propelled gun has been brought into service as an interim until the RCH 155 is fully operational. (MOD/CROWN COPYRIGHT)

BELOW: The Anglo-German RCH 155 will be the Royal Artillery's main close support weapon from 2027. (MOD/CROWN COPYRIGHT)

Challenger 3	
Manufacturer:	RBSL
Unit cost:	£8m
Produced:	2021 to date
Number built:	147 to be built
Specifications	
Mass:	66 tonnes
Length:	8.3m (27ft 3in), 13.5m (44ft 3in)
Width:	3.5m (11ft 6in)
Height:	2.49m (8ft 2in)
Crew:	Four (commander, gunner, loader/operator, driver)
Main armament:	130/120mm Rheinmetall L55A1 smoothbore gun
Secondary armament:	Coaxial 7.62mm L94A1 chain gun EX-34, 7.62mm L37A2 Operator/Loader's hatch machine gun
Engine:	Perkins CV12-9A 26.1 litre V12 diesel
Maximum speed:	59 kph (37mph) on road

RIGHT: The improved Challenger 3 main battle tank is set to enter service from 2027. (MOD/CROWN COPYRIGHT)

In April 2024, the Ministry of Defence announced its selection of the Remote-Controlled Howitzer 155mm (RCH 155) for the British Army's Mobile Fires Platform programme, as a successor for the AS90. The guns will be built in both Germany and the UK with over 100 UK-based suppliers manufacturing components. The weapon is, in effect, a module fitted to a Boxer chassis.

To find targets for this firepower to engage, the Royal Armoured Corps is buying 589 Ajax reconnaissance vehicles. There are six variants of

the Ajax, including reconnaissance, troop carrying, engineer, recovery, repair, and command versions. The project has been delayed by technical problems and the Ministry of Defence now says the first squadron will be ready for action next year and first full regiment will be equipped in 2026.

Air defence has been identified as a critical capability for the British Army and new systems are being bought to fill the gap left by the retirement of legacy Rapier weapon in 2021.

The long-awaited project to provide the Royal Artillery with enough launchers to equip a deployable regiment of Land Ceptors was approved within the Ministry of Defence in November 2023, but contract negotiations with the European guided weapons manufacturer, MBDA, have yet

to conclude. The Land Ceptor is the ground-based variant of the Common Anti-Air Modular Missile (CAMM) that is operational on Royal Navy warships, as Sea Ceptor. An initial batch of launchers have been procured for the Royal Artillery to provide air defence for the Falkland Islands, under the Sky Sabre project. This was a bespoke solution for the Falklands and this new buy is understood to involve new elements that will allow the Royal Artillery air defence regiment to participate in manoeuvre operations.

British Army procurement chiefs are putting the finishing touches to a re-jigged plan to replace their Afghan war-era protected mobility vehicle fleet. The idea is to reduce the projected mobility and utility fleets from 16 to five types of vehicles. This £2.2bn project is

RIGHT: In a major development, the Challenger 3 will be armed with a smooth-barrelled 120mm main armament. (MOD/CROWN COPYRIGHT)

Ajax Armoured Reconnaissance Vehicle	
In service:	Not yet achieved
Used by:	British Army
Manufacturer:	General Dynamics UK
Produced:	2014 to date
Number built:	589 on order
Specifications (Turreted variant)	
Mass:	38 tonnes with growth potential to 42 tonnes
Length:	7.62m (25ft)
Width:	3.35m (11ft)
Height:	3m (9ft 10in)
Crew:	Three plus seven passengers for PMRS variant
Main armament:	CTA International CT40 40mm (1.6in) cannon
Secondary armament:	L94A1 coaxial 7.62mm chain gun, with Kongsberg Protector Remote Weapon Station
Engine:	MTU Friedrichshafen V8
Maximum speed:	70kph

intended to run over the next decade. It aims to replace the Mastiff, Husky, and Wolfhound Mine Resistance Ambush Protected (MRAPs), Combat Reconnaissance Vehicle (Tracked) and Stormer family of tracked vehicles, also being replaced will be Jackal/Coyote patrol vehicles, FV 432 series tracked armoured vehicles, Panther utility vehicles, Land Rover Revised Weapons Mounted Installation Kit vehicles, and Pinzgauer high-mobility all-terrain vehicle, as well as Fuchs specialist armoured troop carriers. This involves several hundred vehicles, but they would not be replaced on a one for one basis.

Army officers say this is not a development programme and said it would involve commercial off the shelf (COTS) and modified off the shelf (MTOS), with prove technology that exists today. The approach would not involve a 'big bang' but a gradual transition, with older and more expensive to support vehicles going out of service quickly but newer vehicles, such as the Foxhound, might be upgraded to allow them to remain in service for a limited period.

The Royal Artillery is replacing its existing mini uncrewed aerial systems (MUAS), such as Desert Hawk 3, with 159 rotary-wing Indago 4 and 105 fixed-wing Stalker VXE30 drones,

which are both capable of locating and identifying targets far from the operator. They are scheduled to be operational by the end of 2024.

Weighing a little over 20kg and with a 4.88m wingspan, the portable Stalker is an operationally proven, vertical-launched, near-silent drone providing more than eight hours of imaging capability and able to cover around 60 miles.

The Indago 4, weighing only 2.27kg, can be folded, and carried in a soldier's backpack and deployed in just two minutes with a range of approximately eight miles. Its high-resolution camera systems provide incredible zoom capability to accurately identify people, objects, vehicles and weapons, day, or night. Existing long range Watchkeeper tactical unmanned aerial vehicles are set to be modernised to allow them to fly further behind enemy lines to find targets.

The British Army's modernisation is gaining momentum and over the next few years, its soldiers will soon have their hands on this new kit. It is an exciting time for the British Army.

LEFT: Soldiers of the Royal Regiment of Fusiliers inspect a prototype Boxer vehicle, ahead of the regiment receiving the vehicles during 2025. (MOD/CROWN COPYRIGHT)

BELOW: Bomb disposal robots have been widely used by the British Army since the 1970s and they have shown the potential for more robotic combat systems. (MOD/CROWN COPYRIGHT)

Fighting Future Wars

How 21st Century Battlefields are Rapidly Changing

A decade ago, British troops were just finishing their eight-year-long mission in Afghanistan's Helmand province that left more than 400 of our soldiers dead. The Taliban's weapon of choice was the improvised bombs, many made from scrap mobile phone components. It was very rare for Taliban fighters to take on British troops in stand-up fights. Those that did were soon silenced by overwhelming British firepower. If any British soldiers were wounded in these skirmishes, a helicopter would be rustled up to lift the casualties to safety in hospital. British forces lost on average around one fatality a week during the guerrilla war in Helmand.

Fast forward to the battlefields of Gaza and Ukraine in 2024 and those wars are of totally a different scale and intensity. The Ukrainians and Russians often lose as many dead or wounded in a single day as the British Army lost in eight years fighting in Helmand. Much of Gaza looks like it has been flattened. All the weapons and tactics used to fight the war in Helmand appear from a different age.

Hundreds of thousands of Russians and Ukrainian troops are now locked in a face off along 1,000 miles of trench lines, sheltering in deep dugouts in summer and winter to survive. This is a brutal and deadly struggle, under non-stop artillery fire. Soldiers dare not emerge from their trenches for fear of attracting a barrage of enemy shells. Tanks and heavy armoured vehicles do not risk breaking cover in case they are hit. It is not even safe in the skies above thanks to the presence of phalanx of anti-aircraft missiles that bring down any aircraft or helicopters that venture into range.

Battlefields have always been cruel, but the Gaza and Ukraine wars have taken it to a new level. The key lessons are that it is just too unhealthy for real humans to venture on to modern battlefields. Drones – air, land and sea-based – are one of the few ways for armed forces to take the war to the enemy without suffering heavy losses.

What has made the battlefields of Ukraine and Gaza so dystopian is the use of tens of thousands of so-called 'hobby drones' to monitor battlefields, 24/7. These can take off

from a palm of a soldier's hand or be fired into the air by catapult. They are often made in China and bought over the internet for as little as $50. These keep every part of the battle under continuous surveillance and as soon as enemy soldiers or vehicles break cover, artillery fire or armed 'kamikaze' drones are aimed at them. Soldiers who get careless can be dead in a matter of minutes. Ukrainian

soldiers and Hamas fighters have even taken to turning their hobby drones into deadly weapons by strapping hand grenades to them. They then fly these into enemy trenches or open hatches of tanks, before detonating the grenades.

The Israeli military has taken this approach one step further with their Lavender intelligence tool. This uses AI to pick up mobile phone

or internet activity by anyone on their intelligence database linked to Hamas. So, if any are stupid enough to switch on their mobile phones or go online, they will be pin-pointed and then killed by missiles fired from drones, all within a matter of minutes.

To survive in this deadly environment, armies are looking to remove the need for human soldiers to venture on to modern »

ABOVE: Russian attack helicopters and 'kamikaze' drones devastated Ukrainian armoured columns when they tried to advance in the summer of 2023. (JULIAN ROEPCKE)

LEFT: The RCH 155 155mm self-propelled howitzer will enable the Royal Artillery to dominate future battlefields. (MOD/CROWN COPYRIGHT)

ABOVE: Ukrainian towns and cities have been devastated by Russian artillery fire over the past two years. (UKRAINIAN MOD)

RIGHT: Armed robot vehicles are set to dominate future battlefields. (MOD/CROWN COPYRIGHT)

battlefields. Future soldiers are being provided with their own robot dogs or mini-tracked drones to move remote control cameras and machine guns to the frontline. The soldiers who do have to risk moving into sight of the enemy will be provided with super-efficient body armour for protection mounted on exoskeletons to cope with the weight.

To counter-this 'all seeing battlefield eye', armies are fielding jamming systems to blind enemy drones by blocking their radio control frequencies. Britain's jammer is called the ORCUS counter drone system, and it is operated by the RAF Regiment. New jammers are being bought for the Royal Signals.

Incorporating Artificial Intelligence (AI) into military command systems is heralded as the holy grail of future warfare. Commanders want to achieve instant reactions to huge enemy drone and missile swarms. AI is already in use and was at the heart of the Israeli defence shield that defeated the massed Iranian drone and missile strike in April. Its AI algorithms allowed the 350 Iranian missiles and drones to be rapidly detected and their flight paths predicted. This then enabled Israeli interceptor missiles to be sent against all the in-bound weapons.

jamming or operator error each week. To keep up with demand, both sides in the Ukraine war have ordered thousands from Chinese factories, which are struggling to build them fast enough.

Future drone war concepts will have to be predicated on having a large supply of replacement drones at hand. So, whoever can build factories that can turn out tens of thousands of cheap drones each month will win future wars. In 2023, the Russians have opened a new 'state of the art' drone factory in Tatarstan that has been assembling 6,000 Iranian-designed drones a year. This has given them a huge drone advantage over the Ukrainians.

Wars have a way of 'testing to destruction' politicians', generals', and scientists' pet theories. When the British Army was fighting in Afghanistan, few of the soldiers patrolling Helmand province would have imagined that $50 Chinese-made drones and $2,000 artillery shells would soon be dominating warfare.

In a matter of weeks, the Ukraine war had turned into a stalemate thanks to the combination of improvised drones and massed artillery fire. Soldier in trenches created their own weapons with a speed that Western defence companies would struggle to rival. It was often said in jest that many Cold War era weapons were purposely designed never to be used in battle. Modern weapon designers are finding their products are being tested in battle for real, sooner than expected. Their failings are rapidly exposed and there are no corporate lobbyists on the battlefield to protect their reputations.

LEFT: The British Army is testing mini-drones that can move around buildings without being noticed. (MOD/CROWN COPYRIGHT)

BELOW: The British Army Experimental Battalion travelled to the United States for several weeks in early to test new robot technology in simulated battles. (MOD/CROWN COPYRIGHT)

Israeli commanders watched the Iranian attack develop in their computerised command post. Within minutes their AI offered up options to counter the attack. The Israelis then picked the best intercept solution, keeping a 'human in the loop'. In future battles involving hundreds more missiles and drones, fired at shorter ranges, commanders might not have the luxury of having time to contemplate what to do. Passing control to AI command systems is a step too far for many nations. In the future, armed forces might be forced to counter the enemy's AI controlled drone swarm with fully AI controlled defensives. This would be robot warfare in its extreme form.

In World War Two, US President Franklin D Roosevelt coined the phrase, "arsenal of democracy" to motivate America's workers to build the tanks, planes, and ships needed to defeat Nazi Germany and imperial Japan.

The idea of building factories to outproduce your enemy's defence industry is suddenly back in fashion.

Drones have transformed warfare. Ukrainian and Russian commanders treat them as 'disposable' items. Hundreds are lost to enemy fire,

Marching into the Future

A British Army for the 21st Century

More soldiers are still leaving the army than are being recruited. Much like the rest of the country, Britain's soldiers need a pay rise after years of below inflation increases in their salaries. Action needs to be taken on the state of crumbling barracks and family houses on army garrisons. These are all quick wins for the new government. Keeping highly trained soldiers in the ranks is a priority and would stop the fortune spent on training them being wasted. Without skilled and resourceful soldiers, the British Army will not be firing on all cylinders.

ABOVE: Cadets at the Royal Military Academy Sandhurst are the future leaders of the British Army. (MOD/CROWN COPYRIGHT)

As *British Army Yearbook 2024* goes to print the country will be voting for a new government. Both major parties, Conservative and Labour, are promising to boost defence spending, although at different rates. There appears to be cross party consensus that the world is more dangerous, with threats from Russia, China, Iran, and other rogue states proliferating.

Whoever wins the election will be faced with a bulging in-tray and the new defence secretary will have to get to work very quickly after moving into his office on the fifth floor of the Ministry of Defence Main Building.

There to greet the new defence secretary will be the new chief of the general staff, General Sir Roly Walker, who will have to brief him on the state of the British Army.

Top of General Walker's to do list will be turning around the British Army's recruiting and retention crisis. At the beginning of April 2024, the force had 72,510 trained regular soldiers and 24,070 trained army reservists. This was under the Future Soldier personnel target of 73,000 regular soldiers that was to have been reached by 2025.

RIGHT: The British Army remains on duty around the world. (MOD/CROWN COPYRIGHT)

There was much conversation during the election campaign about proposals for 18-year-old Britons to do a year of National Service. This followed on from suggestions from the former head of the British Army, General Sir Patrick Sanders, in January that society should be fully mobilised in time of war.

Concern about Russian sabotage across Europe in recent months has piqued interest in what is called 'total defence' in Scandinavia. Finland, Norway, and Sweden all have plans to mobilise tens of thousands of reservists and home guard volunteers to protect bridges, strategic factories, government buildings, and power stations from sabotage in time of war. All these countries have well established civil defence organisations, backed up by thousands of volunteers, to protect their populations against natural disasters, enemy air attacks, power cuts and breakdowns in communications. These measures provide resilience and prevent enemies stoking confusion and panic in a crisis.

The Ministry of Defence is working on a National Defence and Resilience Plan for Britain, and this is supposed to be ready later this year. It is expected that the British Army could have a central role in these new plans. First of all, this is expected to involve establishing a new network of command posts to direct operations in time of war. Army Reserve units are likely to be given new roles protecting vital infrastructure. During the Cold War, the then Territorial Army had a major role in home defence to protect key points around Britain from Soviet sabotage. The Army Reserve is well placed to take on this task again if a future government wants to think again about defending the British homeland.

Continuing wars in Ukraine, the Middle East, and Africa are expected to continue to result in calls for the British

Army to help out. The British Army's ongoing support to train and equip the Ukraine military is likely to continue, with Kyiv's soldiers coming to Britain to be drilled. Some NATO countries have proposed sending instructing teams into Ukraine to speed up the training of its army, but British ministers have not yet endorsed this idea.

The Gaza crisis has led to instability across the Middle East, and this has seen the British Army called to help protect allied forces in the region. This has resulted in soldiers from air defence, counter-drone, intelligence, and radar units deploying in small teams in Iraq, Syria, and Saudi Arabia. Training teams from the Ranger Regiment have also been very active, helping allies and partners to respond to attacks from Iran and its allies. These 'below the radar' operations are giving British ministers increased influence in the region and an enhanced understanding of emerging threats.

In this complex and fast-moving environment, the British Army is proving it is relevant to the 21st century and coming up with new ways of protecting British interests.

Over the past four years, the British Army has undergone dramatic changes. Few expect that this period of change is over. General Walker and his new top team will have to deal with even more uncertainty and change over the coming years. The Britain Army has long a had the unofficial motto, 'adapt, improvise and overcome'.